21131314G

21131314G

D0296882

2002

FEB 2004

D13 4+

starcniit

THERE'S ONLY ONE
DAVID
BECKHAM

THERE'S ONLY ONE
DAVID
BECKHAM

STAFFORD HILDRED
AND TIM EWBANK

JOHN BLAKE

796.33

2113131 4G

CLACKMANNANSHIRE
LIBRARIES

WITHDRAWN

F

Published by John Blake Publishing Ltd, 3 Bramber Court,
2 Bramber Road, London W14 9PB, England

First published in hardback in 2002

ISBN 1 904034 05 5

All rights reserved. No part of this publication may be reproduced,
stored in a retrieval system, or in any form or by any means, without
the prior permission in writing of the publisher, nor be otherwise circulated in any form
of binding or cover other than that in which it is published and without a similar
condition including this condition
being imposed on the subsequent purchaser.

British Library Cataloguing-in-Publication Data: A catalogue record
for this book is available from the British Library.

Design by ENVY

Printed and bound in Great Britain by CPD (Wales)

1 3 5 7 9 10 8 6 4 2

© Text copyright Stafford Hildred and Tim Ewbank 2002

Papers used by John Blake Publishing Ltd are natural, recyclable products
made from wood grown in sustainable forests. The manufacturing processes conform to
the environmental regulations of the country of origin.

Every attempt has been made to contact the relevant copy-right holders, but some
where unobtainable. We would be grateful if the appropriate people could contact us.

CONTENTS

Stafford Hildred would like to dedicate this book to Janet, Claire and Rebecca, and to all survivors of the East Lincs Combination.

Tim Ewbank would like to dedicate this book to Oliver.

ACKNOWLEDGEMENTS

The authors would like to thank David Beckham for his inspirational leadership; and also the many fans, admirers, friends, associates and acquaintances of David Beckham who spoke to us for this book.

PROLOGUE

DAVID BECKHAM has a happy habit of making dreams come true. On October 6, 2001 as England's final World Cup qualifier drifted agonisingly into the third minute of injury time, it looked as if all the heroics in Munich were going to be in vain. Germany were drawing with Finland and England were 2-1 down to the Greeks – and if those scores still stood at the final whistle, it would be Germany who would snatch the automatic qualification place for the World Cup, leaving England to struggle through a further play-off round...

England's captain was leading by example in a terrific all-action performance, but his team was finding it hard going coping with their nerves and a Greek side that was playing well for its pride. As the minutes ticked away, the situation increasingly frustrated skipper and team alike. Beckham had already seen a series of eight flashing free-kicks fail to find the net and when he put the ball down for the last throw of the dice, Teddy Sheringham stepped up to offer his services.

But this was definitely a captain's job and Beckham felt that, at just short of 30 yards, this free-kick was a little too far out for his old club-mate. He placed the ball and the nation held its breath as he eased into that familiar athletic run to the ball. He struck it as sweetly as Tiger Woods times a crucial seven-iron and there was a wonderful feeling of warm inevitability as the ball arced away from the flailing Greek goalkeeper and into the corner of the net.

David Beckham will surely score many more fine goals in his remarkable career but it's hard to believe he will ever manage a more dramatic strike than that free-kick (clocked at an average speed of 64.8 mph). He turned back with a shining smile of sheer delight and the country smiled back. Goldenballs, as his wife Victoria so appropriately calls him,

> ⚽ **Goldenballs, as his wife Victoria so appropriately calls him, had done it again.**

had done it again. It seemed so fitting that the man whose moment of indiscretion in France arguably ended England's last attempt to win the last World Cup had so brilliantly kick-started the last vital leap into the next competition.

But then David Beckham's whole life is the story of dreams coming true. As a young boy his every waking thought was of playing football. He was fortunate to be born into a warm and loving family with highly supportive parents. His mum and dad carefully nurtured his young ambitions without ever putting too much pressure on their clearly gifted son to succeed. David's father, Ted, was an enthusiastic local footballer who was delighted when he recognised early signs that his son might well have special talents. But he carefully refrained from pushing David too hard too soon. Too many young talents founder because of pushy parents and the Beckham Junior was gently encouraged to develop a love for football. And his undying passion for 'the beautiful game', coupled with sublime natural skills, has made him probably the most famous footballer in the world today.

This is the story of how those young dreams became a reality.

CHAPTER 1

GROWING UP

DAVID ROBERT Joseph Beckham was born in Leytonstone, east London on May 2, 1975. From a young age he loved to kick a football around, and as far back as he can remember there was only one team he ever wanted to play for: Manchester United. As a boy, David loved to watch his father play football and he yearned to be given a chance to join in. But Ted Beckham was determined to look after his son and refused to let him play until he was ready. David practised his football for hours, often under the protective eye of his father. Every aspect of the game – from passing and shooting to trapping the ball and tackling – would feature in these early training sessions. As soon as he got home from school David would rush off to his local Chase Lane park for a kick around. Often there would be games with his friends, but if he was alone he would practise rigorously at keeping the ball in the air. The skills that grace Old Trafford might sometimes look simply God-given, but they were nurtured in hours of dedicated application.

Advert in Chingford local paper: 'WANTED – Football superstars of the future. Only talented boys need apply. Box 416'. David Beckham was one of 43 boys who applied to that advertisement placed by Stuart Underwood, manager of local side Ridgeway Rovers, for players for his Under-8 team. 'Chase Lane Park is where we started and that's about 200 yards from David's house,' explains Stuart. 'So he heard about it and came over. He could knock the ball in from a corner right into the middle of the goal without any effort at all. He had the ability to strike the ball perfectly.'

> '**WANTED –** Football superstars of the future. Only talented boys need apply. Box 416'

The wider world first learned of David Beckham when he was just 11 years old. David saw a Bobby Charlton Soccer Skills School mentioned on Blue Peter and asked his mother if he could go on it. He entered the initial competition and came top with 1,106 points, going on to finish first in the whole competition out of 5,000 young footballing hopefuls. The famous Bobby Charlton name had helped to focus David on a future at Old Trafford, but he was also to visit another soccer centre of excellence – his prize included a trip to visit Barcelona, then managed by Terry Venables.

Despite his youth, he soon found himself showing off his ball skills on television, on a show called *Daytime* with Sarah Kennedy. Even in those early days, David demonstrated he had an astonishingly powerful right foot. Young contemporaries would watch in open-mouthed amazement as he floated over a pin-point accurate corner, or let fly with one of his full-blooded free-kicks that had goalkeepers going weak at the knees.

Remember that awesome David Beckham goal against Wimbledon a few years ago? Well, even as a 13-year-old David managed to score from the halfway line and when he joined newly formed local side Ridgeway Rovers, he was soon at the heart of a remarkable early success story: the side went 90 games without defeat.

David and his two sisters at the wedding of his sister Lynne.

David has two sisters. His older sister Lynne would fiercely stand up for her gifted brother at school, though she did not share his passion for football.

But his younger sister Joanne loved football and was frequently involved in his early practice sessions. David was highly gifted at other sports at school too. He played everything from rounders to rugby, and as well as his prowess as a footballer he really shone as an athlete. He was excellent at cross country running at school and he was county 1,500 metres champion for four years running.

> A description of nine-year-old David in a cup programme when he was playing for Ridgeway Rovers, sums him up as: 'Tricky winger. Football-mad. Played with Club since formed. Also plays for Waltham Forest District.'

But there was only ever one sport for the young Beckham. As a teenager, football seemed to dominate David's every waking moment. His earliest experience of top live games came with visits to White Hart Lane to see Tottenham, when his dad managed to get tickets, though they also watched West Ham and Arsenal. Although there was no shortage of London clubs for David to admire, however, his heart was always in Old Trafford. He liked the other clubs all right, but he loved Manchester United. It was as simple as that.

David was never in any real trouble as a youngster, but he wasn't exactly good as gold. His mother Sandra recalled that David was never naughty when he was growing up, except for the time he had his ear pierced at the age of 14. (Sandra told him not to have it done, but he had it pierced anyway.)

As a youngster he might have preferred watching *Match of the Day* to going out and hanging around street corners with some of his friends, but he did stay out too late more than once. When he did break the rules, the punishment would be strict but fair. He would be stopped from going to football training – and that punishment hit David harder than anything else could have.

> David Beckham told schoolchildren in Stockport at a launch of Adidas' Team Football initiative that he might have been an artist if he hadn't found fame on the football pitch. David said: 'I would have enjoyed lessons at school more if we talked about football, but I was quite good at art. Maybe I would have gone into that if I had not got my break into soccer.'

The teenager David's first part-time job was as a potboy and washer-up in the bar at Walthamstow Greyhound Stadium. 'He used to get paid £3 a night for collecting glasses and fetching bottles,' remembers regular Diane Gleeson. 'It was his job to clean the pumps at the end of the night and to make sure the wines and spirits didn't run out in the bar. He was a lovely lad, always very smart and well presented. People used to think he was shy because he would sometimes blush if the customers teased him. But I gradually realised he could handle himself in any situation.

'There was one very regular lady customer who took a

real shine to him,' Diane recalls. 'She was old enough to be his mum but I don't think she was feeling maternal towards him at all, because he was very good looking, even when he was 14. One night this lady had drunk a couple of brandy and sodas too many and she was a bit rude to David. I overheard her telling him it was about time he found out what it was like to spend a night with a good woman. I thought, *Oh blimey, what next*, but I was behind the bar and I couldn't get out to intervene. David just said, "Yes I'd love to come round to your place after I finish work. Can I bring my mum and dad?" She got the message straight away and shut up.

'David was like that. He looked like a little lad but he was very mature and grown up underneath. We knew he was a good footballer because even then he had a reputation after being on telly as a kid. But he never bragged or boasted and whenever customers would bore on about West Ham or whatever he was always very polite.'

David's excellent sporting ability shone out in his school reports too, though judging from the following comments, his attention often wandered:

'DAVID HAS A NATURAL ABILITY TO SUCCEED AT MOST SPORTS. BUT HE SHOULD BE CAREFUL OF DISTRACTIONS WHICH AFFECT HIS APPLICATION.'

(Comments by Chingford School's PE teacher on David's school report, July 1987)

'DAVID HAS ABILITY BUT HE FINDS IT DIFFICULT TO CONCENTRATE. HIS ATTITUDE MUST IMPROVE IMMEDIATELY IF HE IS TO FULFIL HIS POTENTIAL.'

(David's Chingford School report from his Humanities teacher, 1987)

TRIED TO BEHAVE AS HE'S ON REPORT. HOWEVER HE LAPSED INTO HIS USUAL SILLY BEHAVIOUR, FOOLING WITH OTHER CLASS MEMBERS WHILE WASHING UP. COOKED GOOD CAKES.'

(Home Economics teacher's report, autumn term 1989)

Nana Boachie is a big Beckham fan and says he'll never forget the future star's first competitive league goal – because he was the keeper who let the ball slip through his fingers! The two were 11-year-old schoolboys at the time, and good friends. But friendship was forgotten when the young David Beckham rocketed the ball into the back of Nana's net. 'David was always good at shots and free-kicks around the area,' recalls Nana, who was playing for the Grasshoppers against Beckham's Ridgeway Rovers. 'In fact, free-kicks were like penalties to him because he would

⚽ **We put up a wall but David stepped back and then curled the ball into the top corner.**

always score. It was really miserable weather. The rain was sheeting down and the pitch was so wet the ref almost called the game off. But we were all so keen to play we shouted him out of it. It was the start of our first proper football competition and David desperately wanted to start off with a goal. He was never big-headed, but he was always confident. Even then you could see he was skilful and he could kick a ball much harder than anyone else. We had a laugh that I wanted to keep a clean sheet and he just said, "We'll see", in that quiet voice of his. I knew he meant business. We did keep him out for quite a while but then, just before half-time, we gave away a free-kick just outside the area. David took the ball and measured his run-up…

'I was quite big for my age, so I covered quite a lot of the goal. We put up a wall but David stepped back and then curled the ball into the top corner. I knew exactly what he was going to do [but] It was impossible to save. Although I was very pleased for him as we were mates, I was gutted I didn't get near the ball.' But Beckham's subsequent goal-scoring record has set Nana's mind at rest – now he knows he's not the only one to fall foul of the sharp shooter. And although his own footballing career didn't take off, he is delighted for his old friend. 'Whenever I look at the television and see David score a goal, I feel excited for him,' says Nana. 'I happened to meet up recently and he was just the same David. He loves football a lot more than everything that goes with it. And he certainly remembered that first fabulous free-kick!'

Schoolfriend Ryan Kirby played in many early games

alongside David Beckham. 'David used to be a bit mouthy with the big kids when he first started playing,' he recalls. 'They wanted to kick him because he was so skilful. Most of the time he would let the swearing and the abuse slide right over him but he would also give it back. We had to tell him to shut up sometimes because he could get into trouble.' The big game of the year for David's school was the annual fixture

⚽ **Even when he trained as a boy with Spurs, David used to wear a Manchester United shirt.**

against local rivals Tom Wood School. Right-back Kirby was the minder assigned to protect his pal: 'That was a bit of a rough school and they had a few hard players playing for them,' he explains. 'Dave used to look forward to that game in particular because it was a real local derby. At school all me and David would ever tell the careers teacher is that we wanted to become professional footballers. As we grew up more and more of our mates fell away and gave up on it but we stuck firm to our ambitions. Unfortunately, mine never quite worked out but I still love the game as much as David.'

Martin Heather was one of David Beckham's early football coaches for Waltham Forest Under-12s and the Essex county side. He was appalled when the England selectors ruled him out of the national side because of his size. Martin says: 'David got through to the last 70 who went for trials in Nottingham but I was told there was no way he was going to make it because he was too small. Obviously skill and ability had nothing to do with it! I hope those selectors have watched him since.'

It still irritates fans of both Tottenham Hotspur and West

Ham United that David, a boy from Leytonstone, did not end up either as a Hammer or a Spurs player. Even when he trained as a boy with Spurs, David used to wear a Manchester United shirt. That was the team he always loved and always wanted to play for.

His allegiance to Manchester United was cemented when he won that Bobby Charlton TSB Soccer Skills Final at Old Trafford in December 1986. David dazzled a packed crowd with his skills at passing, dribbling, and shooting. Spurs fan Ian Jones recalls those early glimpses of Beckham brilliance: 'I was at Old Trafford supporting Spurs on the day they had the finals of the Bobby Charlton Soccer Coaching School skills contest. When they announced that the winner was a kid called David Beckham from Essex, all the Spurs fans started chanting his name, thinking that he must be a Tottenham fan. Then it was announced that this kid was a Man U fan and we all started to boo. Can you imagine it? David Beckham getting booed for the first time in his life at the age of 11 – and at Old Trafford of all places!'

⚽ **Manchester United's revered elder statesman knew as soon as he saw the 11-year-old David Beckham kick the ball that he was different.**

Bobby Charlton first saw David Beckham when he was a pupil at one of his famous soccer schools at Hopwood Hall in Manchester. Manchester United's revered elder statesman knew as soon as he saw the 11-year-old David Beckham kick the ball that he was different. David's natural touch and feel for the game shone through, even at that age. He had tremendous technique, wonderful balance, and natural

The great
Bobby
Charlton.

competitiveness. Bobby Charlton has watched with enormous pleasure and satisfaction as the Beckham talent has blossomed at Old Trafford. 'If he has a secret,' Charlton says, 'it is that he has retained his hunger to be the best. That is a quality I first saw in him as a schoolboy. Probably I saw a lot of myself in him as a boy, with his love of the game and the overwhelming desire to be a footballer. He is a perfectionist who often stays behind after training to practise his dead ball work.

> **'If you stuck a girl or a ball in front of David, he'd pick up the ball.'**
>
> John Bullock, David Beckham's school games teacher

'David will tie a rubber tyre to a crossbar and then take 50 free-kicks from either side of the pitch, aiming to hit the ball through the tyre,' Charlton reveals. 'He's athletic, possesses immense running power and stamina and thankfully he rarely gets injured. Great players don't come along too often, but when they do they are a joy to watch.'

> **'He was an outstandingly talented individual. Fortunately he has gone on to realise his talent and do very well. He was very dedicated, very focused, excellent attitude, and really he deserves everything he's got.'**
>
> Martin Heather, Manager Essex Schools 1986–90.

Years later, David selected a poem for a book called *Hug O'War* which was compiled to raise money to help orphans in Kosovo. He picked 'Hey Diddle Diddle' and like other stars he wrote his choice out in his own handwriting and revealed a childhood memory.

He recalled the time when, as a 12-year-old, he heard that a Manchester United scout had spotted him and he cried.

But although David Beckham's natural talent won him many admirers early on, not everyone saw him as a future footballing phenomenon just waiting to explode. Soccer agent Eric Hall still regrets the day he missed out his share of the Beckham millions. He took a telephone call from proud father Ted Beckham who wanted advice on the best deal for his promising son and Eric promised to ring back. To his eternal regret he forgot and although he still handles the careers of Premiership stars such as Dennis Wise and Robbie Savage, he missed out on his chance of signing up Britain's number one player. 'It was one of those terribly busy days,' recalls Eric who was in the middle of several important negotiations for his clients. Eric receives lots of calls from dads hoping he will be the agent to steer their sons the right way and he always tries to help. But Eric is happy to admit that David Beckham was one budding superstar he missed out on and every time he sees David hammer in another wonderful goal, he wonders what might have been if only he'd phoned Ted Beckham back.

CHAPTER 2

MAN U THROUGH AND THROUGH

There's only one Old Trafford – the scene of some of David's finest moments.

DAVID HAD a close relationship with Manchester United throughout his teenage years. The club were well aware of the potential of the lad with the spiky hairstyle who had won the Soccer Skills contest. Bobby Charlton was always insistent that boys who succeeded in his Soccer Skills School were free to join the club of their choice, but David Beckham only ever wanted to play for Manchester United. David was even the mascot for one fixture at West Ham and he watched his beloved Manchester United at every opportunity. The senior players took a shine to the fresh-faced youngster from London who couldn't wait to grow up and join them. Skipper Steve Bruce recalls that David was teased mercilessly on one highly privileged visit to the dressing room, but took the ribbing in exactly the right way.

⚽ **David Beckham only ever wanted to play for Manchester United.**

David signed for Manchester United on his 14th birthday, May 2, 1989. It was the proudest moment of his young life as Alex Ferguson welcomed him to the famous club and David felt that all his dreams were finally coming true. It took a big effort on his part to convince himself that it really was happening. David still had his bedroom wall adorned with posters of his hero, Bryan Robson. He was the proud owner of a shirt with Robson's name on it and now he was to be a player at the very same club. After years of striving towards his goal, David certainly had to pinch himself to make sure he was still in the real world.

⚽ **His closest and most enduring friendship was with defender Gary Neville.**

He quickly made friends with other young hopefuls such as Ryan Giggs, Paul Scholes, Lee Sharpe and Nicky Butt, but his closest and most enduring friendship was with defender Gary Neville. The two lads both came from strong and supportive families and found they shared many values as well as ambitions. Of course, the young players lived in digs in the years before their million-pound contracts arrived. David moved a couple of times but soon found himself happily billeted with a down-to-earth couple called Tommy and Annie Kay who made sure he felt at home. He stayed there for more than two years and received an excellent initial grounding and a secure home that enabled him to concentrate fully on his football. That said, leaving home and going to live in Manchester was one of the strangest experiences of David's life. 'It is a daunting feeling when you are 16, leaving home and coming up to a strange place,' he recalled, years later. There were plenty of new challenges for him to face, but David was anxious to make a success of moving up to Manchester to play for his beloved United. He knew a lot of people were unsure about whether

'It was weird, like stepping from London into Coronation Street.'

David Beckham, on his move up to Manchester

he would be able to make the big jump from living happily at home, but he was determined not to come home with his tail between his legs.

When David went to Manchester United, he wasn't as tall as his mother Sandra. (She is five feet four inches.) In fact David's slight frame and lack of real physical presence on the pitch led to other youngsters, such as Nicky Butt and Gary

Bryan Robson, one of David's idols.

Neville, making an impact on the first team before him. But David Beckham kept growing right to the end of his teens and his physique really began to fill out after lots of dedicated work in the gym with weights.

Today David Beckham can often be found passing on nuggets of knowledge to eager youngsters. He remembers his early days at Old Trafford with affection because first team heroes like Bryan Robson and Steve Bruce were so helpful to him back then. David and the other young recruits were made to feel part of the Old Trafford family from the start and he will be forever grateful for that. And the results were quickly evident on the pitch.

David took his place in an impressive Manchester United youth side that went on to win the FA Youth Cup in 1992.

David made his first team debut for Manchester United in September 1992 when he came on as substitute in a League Cup game away against Brighton. He was just 17 years old and even though

> **'You could always see he had an outstanding talent. The problem he was going to have was that he was very, very small. Bryan Robson said to him: "Drink Guinness and milk, it'll make you grow." He grew to six foot one, so I'm more than pleased for him.'**
>
> Steve Kirby, Ridge Rovers Trainers
> 1983–1986

> **'From day one his talent had to be seen to be believed. There's no doubt he will go on to become one of the most dominant players in English football.'**
>
> Eric Harrison, Manchester United
> youth coach, 1995

he had been doing well in the reserves he was not expecting to be brought on in the first team. He had travelled down to the south coast seaside resort in a terrifyingly tiny plane and arrived at the impressive Grand Hotel for the night match. David was full of nerves when he was brought on for Andrei Kanchelskis but he acquitted himself well.

Manager Alex Ferguson was well aware of the towering potential of the young David Beckham, but he shrewdly decided he needed more first team experience – and that would be some time coming at Old Trafford. So, in March 1995, David was allowed to go out on loan to Preston North End, where Ferguson knew he would continue his education in the school of hard knocks and come back a better player. David was hardly over the moon at the prospect. Manchester United meant more to

> **'Ask football fans who is the most famous player ever to play for Preston North End and most people will say Tom Finney. But what people forget is that David had a few games for Preston on loan from Manchester United.'**
>
> Johnny Scratchley, Preston fan

him than anything else in the world and he was worried that the players who were in line to be unloaded were frequently the ones to be loaned out – to put them in soccer's shop window, so to speak. But Alex Ferguson explained to David that he was most definitely not on his way out of Old Trafford on a permanent basis. It was simply that the manager knew the youngster could have a few games in the Third Division and come back a better player.

David did not want to be seen as a big-time Charlie who was lowering himself to play with a smaller club, and so he took on the challenge of playing for Preston North End wholeheartedly. For starters, he volunteered to train with the Preston players when he could have done his training with Manchester United – something that seemed to go down well with his new team-mates. He was helped by the manner of his arrival in the team. And to the delight of manager Gary Peters, he scored direct from a corner in his very first game. In the next match, David hammered home a trademark free-kick against Fulham that helped Preston to a victory. The youngster's obvious skill and high level of enthusiasm really lifted all the other players.

Gary Peters confirms that David's spell with his team added a vital ingredient of toughness to his game. 'Alex Ferguson believed that the only thing missing from his game was the physical aspect,' Gary recalls. 'There was no questioning his ability, but they didn't believe he got stuck in enough. Fergie quickly agreed to us taking him on loan and said he thought it would do the lad some good. He knew we played a passing game but he was also aware that you have to stand up to the physical rigours, too. I was a bit worried that David would struggle with the physical side. At this level you have to win the ball first and that means scrapping for it. At first I had to bully and cajole him a bit. But David soon got the message that he had to mix it with the hard nuts and he learned very quickly.

'The fans just loved him,' Gary recalls, warmly. 'I knew his passing was excellent and his shooting was outstanding but he even shocked me when he scored direct from a corner against Doncaster. It was no fluke. He hit it with such pace and accuracy the keeper didn't have a chance. Then he scored with a free-kick against Fulham that was pure class. It was a wicked bender and you knew you were watching someone very special.

United watched every one of his five games for us so I was not surprised when Alex Ferguson rang and said he was taking him back. Alex knew that David had found the physical side to his game and threw him into the first team. Alex knew very well what he had in Beckham and he kept an eye on him when he played for us.'

> 'David learned 99 per cent of what he knows from United, but I like to believe that the missing one per cent was gained at Preston.'
>
> Gary Peters, Preston North End manager

But even if David Beckham was always only a temporary player at Preston North End, Gary feels he picked up something valuable during his brief stay. 'We helped his education in that he became tougher, more competitive and resilient,' he insists, 'and ultimately he gained even more from the loan spell that we did. We had a big hole when he left but I still get a buzz when I watch him and he keeps in touch. He came over when we won promotion and he is a genuine nice guy. He has grafted and now he is getting the rewards. It was just a pity we couldn't keep him.'

After five games for Preston David was a new hero in the town, but Alex Ferguson quickly re-called him to more serious action. And David certainly noticed the difference.

Ooh, aah, Cantona! Eric has a kickaround on the beach.

One Saturday he had lined up at Lincoln City in front of a tiny crowd and the next week he was playing against Leeds United with more than 40,000 fans screaming for victory. It was quite a change. By the end of the season, though, David had still played in more league games for Preston than he had for Manchester United.

Blackburn Rovers just beat the Reds to the title that year. But as the momentous 1995/96 season began, manager Ferguson started to ring the changes. Mark Hughes, Paul Ince and Andrei Kanchelskis were allowed to leave Old Trafford and that opened up the opportunity in midfield for younger players such as David Beckham to make their mark. After an early setback against Aston Villa, BBC commentator Alan Hansen famously sneered that you could not win anything with kids. That was exactly the sort of remark to make the United players all the more determined to succeed. The young side – soon to be dubbed 'Fergie's Fledglings' by the press – turned in an astonishing sequence of fine performances and by the end of the season Manchester United had triumphed in an epic League and FA Cup double. David Beckham played 32 times and scored eight electrifying goals. In the galaxy of old Trafford, a new star had been born.

> 'Eric was my role model. He is the best I've ever played with. A great guy. One day I would like to be as charismatic as him.'
>
> David Beckham

That said, David's career got off to something of an inauspicious start. His first Premiership game for

Manchester United – against Leeds United on April 2, 1995 – was written off by the *Guardian* : 'Although the 19-year-old David Beckham did well on his Premiership debut, he could not be expected to provide the service that Cole has come to expect from Kanchelskis.'

There was plenty of work to do, but there were plenty of inspirational figures on hand – such as Peter Schmeichel and Eric Cantona – to act as wonderful role models for the young players. David was heartened to see that, just like himself, Cantona practised his remarkable skills for hours even after training was over. The precision and power in those feet was honed to perfection with long periods of lonely practice. The charismatic Frenchman was a man of few words, even with his team-mates, but for David Beckham and the rest of the side he did his leading by example. In fact, Eric Cantona was David Beckham's early hero at Manchester United.

THE GREATEST GOAL OF ALL TIME?

There are many who believe that David's Beckham's goal for Manchester United against Wimbledon on August 17, 1996, was the greatest ever seen.

The crowd of 25,786 at Selhurst Park will certainly never forget it. Beckham was just inside his own half when he looked up and spotted Wimbledon's goalkeeper Neil Sullivan a long way off his line. From 55 yards he sent a powerful shot over Sullivan that dipped into the net as the hapless goalie desperately scampered back in vain.

John Motson, commentator on BBC TV's *Match of the Day*, couldn't contain his astonishment at the wonder goal: 'Ohhhhhh! That is absolutely phenomenal!' he gushed. 'David Beckham – surely an England player for the future – scores a goal that will be talked about and replayed for years!' United legend Eric Cantona added his voice to the general praise, by commenting, 'Beautiful goal, David,' which must have made the young Beckham's year!

> **'What can you say? It's the first time I've ever seen a goal scored from someone in his own half.'**
>
> Joe Kinnear, Wimbledon boss.

Brian McClair, who laid on the pass, joked: 'When I finally made my entrance 12 minutes from time United were 2-0 up after goals by Eric Cantona and Dennis Irwin, and all that was necessary was to keep the ball for the short period which remained. David Beckham hadn't picked up on this and he miss-hit a cross from 50 yards and scored a third.'

Alex Ferguson was unstinting in his praise Beckham's strike: 'You have seen the goal of the season,' he stated, flatly. 'I have never seen it done before. Everyone in the dressing room has been scratching their heads trying to think of a goal like it. It was marvellous. A truly tremendous strike. When you have a shot like he has, it will always be worth a try.'

It was no one-off. On October 12, 1996, playing against old rivals Liverpool at Old Trafford, David scored the winning goal with a fierce strike, driving a loose ball past Liverpool goalie David James into the bottom left-hand corner. Sky Sports soccer pundit Andy Gray was impressed: 'You might be six feet five and sprawling across your goal but you're not going to save this,' he marvelled. 'This was gloriously struck. You just don't save them, David James, I'm sorry. What a goal!' Manchester United won 1-0.

David was soon winning a reputation for his penetrating crosses and scintillating work from set pieces. Indeed, he scored with such a fine free-kick for Manchester United against Barcelona at old Trafford in September 1998 that it provoked respectful analysis from two previous masters of the dead ball art. Ronald Koeman, who dashed England's hopes of qualifying for the World Cup in

⚽ **'This was gloriously struck. You just don't save them, David James, I'm sorry. What a goal!'**

the USA in 1994 with an excellent free-kick, said Beckham's strike was one of the best he had ever seen. 'The incredible thing about Beckham's free-kick,' Koeman observed, 'is that he hit it with a mixture of spin and power. It was technically brilliant. But you can't do something like that without constantly practising it in training. He only stepped back one or two yards yet was still able to hit it so powerfully. I would say it was better than his goal in the 1998 World Cup against Colombia because of the mixture of strength and spin. And it is one thing scoring goals like that in training but quite another in a game of such significance.'

Ex-Manchester United winger Gordon Hill, himself the scorer of some fine goals direct from a free-kick, added: 'He

winds up the shot very sharply, like an elastic band. His toes are pointed downwards and away from him rather like a ballet dancer. But he keeps the ball on the inside of his foot as distinct from the top of it. The fact his toes are pointed downwards and away from him gives it that extra curve. There is no way a goalkeeper can stop it if it is struck properly. I was sitting level with where David struck the ball. He used the wind to his advantage. The keeper was slightly off-centre trying to cover both posts. In those circumstances no-one would have stopped it.'

No doubt about it, David Beckham's scintillating free-kicks have thrilled fans right round the world. He often practises free-kicks in bare feet to improve his feel for the ball. 'It's something I always have done,' he says. 'And no, it doesn't damage my feet.'

The abundance of young talent at Old Trafford was soon being reflected in the amount of silverware in Manchester United's trophy cabinet. They had done the double in 1996, picking up the League Championship and the FA Cup, and had won the League again the following season. But it was 1999 that was to be the team's *annus mirabilis*. The season had started badly for David, with his infamous dismissal against Argentina in the World Cup – more of which later. However, by the season's close, he had three glittering trophies to demonstrate his rehabilitation, as Manchester United swept to a tremendous treble.

The League title came first and the FA Cup semi-final against Arsenal was highlighted by a spectacular solo goal from Ryan Giggs, following a 50-yard run. Curiously,

Giggs's elated celebration – sprinting around with his shirt off – lives as long in the memory as the goal itself. United finally clinched the title with a crucial win over Tottenham thanks to goals from Andy Cole and David Beckham.

In the FA Cup Final, Manchester United lined up against Newcastle United and dominated the game after an early goal from Teddy Sheringham. A second came from Paul Scholes and the match was won. David Beckham was moved to the centre of midfield during the game when Roy Keane was forced to go off injured. The players were saddened to lose the services of their inspirational skipper; they knew that he was already ruled out of the European Cup final through suspension. His season was over, but for David Beckham it meant a move to centre stage.

Celebrations for the two domestic triumphs were understandably muted as the team switched its collective concentration to the challenge of facing Bayern Munich in the final of the European Champions Cup, in the fabulous setting of Barcelona's Nou Camp. It was the biggest game of David Beckham's career and he had a terrific match.

⚽ **'He brought me up and has made my career what it is. So we all owe the manager everything.'**

The final produced one of the most dramatic turnarounds in football history. Richard Turner, a lifelong Manchester United supporter, was one of the thousands of fans who travelled to the Nou Camp to witness an incredibly dramatic comeback by his team that night. From his seat, J17 in section B30 on the second tier of the Goal Nord stand, Richard was above and behind the goal where the game's three goals were scored. He had a perfect view of all three. 'Beckham's contribution to the win has possibly been overlooked or underestimated in all the euphoria,' he argues. 'Beckham had extra responsibility resting on his shoulders in midfield for Manchester United, as both Roy Keane and Paul Scholes were ineligible for the game because of suspension. He coped pretty well. What I remember most about Beckham from that game was his sheer never-give-up determination as the game appeared to us thousands of United fans to be slipping away. The 90 minutes were up and Bayern were winning 1-0. I'd taken a day off work,

⚽ **'My nan is always remarking how often I seem to argue with referees.'**

flown out to Barcelona from Luton airport, spent six hours mingling with other Man U supporters and seen the team largely underperform. Now it looked as though the game was lost. It was going to be a depressing journey home.

'Then Beckham epitomised the team's refusal to be beaten. From a throw-in in the 90th minute, Beckham picked up the ball and, still full of running, drove hard along the left, beating two men before slipping the ball wide to Gary Neville. Neville's cross was forced out for the first of Beckham's two perfectly delivered late corners, which led to Teddy Sheringham's equaliser and then Ole Gunnar Solskjaer's winner.' Trailing 1-0 after 90 minutes and 17 seconds, the Red Devils staged one of the most unlikely comebacks in footballing history when, at 90 minutes and 35 seconds, Teddy Sheringham scored following a corner from David Beckham that had been only half-cleared.

After 92 minutes and 15 seconds, Beckham took another corner. Teddy Sheringham rose to flick it on with his head, and Ole Gunnar Solskjaer, on the edge of the six-yard box, instinctively stuck out a foot and the ball shot into the roof of the net.

Later, David Beckham dedicated the remarkable last-gasp victory to manager Alex Ferguson. 'This is for him,' he said. 'He deserves everything he gets. He brought me up and has made my career what it is. So we all owe the manager everything.'

By the end of the season, the team could be truly proud of their achievements: they had secured the Premiership title, the FA Cup and the European Champions Cup. It had been an immensely satisfying season, packed with the sort of exhilarating football that has made English football and Manchester United so popular around the world.

*   *   *

David Beckham is certainly passionate about his football but he firmly rejects suggestions that he lets his emotions get out of control on the pitch. He plays with 100 per cent commitment because that is what the game demands and in spite of the screaming headlines his disciplinary record is far better that his critics would have us believe. David has been sent off just once in a Manchester United shirt, following a high challenge in Brazil's steamy Maracana stadium in a game against the Mexican side Necaxa. David's foot was high and he had to go, but it was an ill-timed tackle in the heat of the moment rather than the attempted homicide some Beckham baiters seemed to regard it as. (Interestingly, David says his grandmother is one of the most perceptive critics of his footballing performances on the pitch: 'My nan is always remarking how often I seem to argue with referees. Worse than that is that my nan is an excellent lip reader so she knows exactly what I'm saying!')

Manager Alex Ferguson was quick to defend his player on that occasion. Indeed, in spite of the acres of newsprint written about the so-called 'rift' between the two men, the relationship remains close. David has been happy to go on record to affirm that the two most important influences in his life are his father and his Manchester United manager. Ted Beckham instilled in his son the guiding principle of working hard to make the most of his remarkable God-given footballing abilities. Alex Ferguson harnessed those skills to place David Beckham at the nerve centre of one of the most successful soccer sides the world has ever seen.

Of course, there have been differences of opinion. Famously David missed training before a fixture against Leeds United at Elland Road when baby Brooklyn was taken ill in the night. He alerted the coaching staff to his impending absence, but manager Ferguson was not pleased and sparks flew when the two men met next day. David was horrified at the thought that he had somehow let down his team-mates because he had acted with the natural anxious concern of a new father. But Alex Ferguson is the boss and he made his point by leaving David Beckham watching

David incurred the wrath of mentor Alex Ferguson when he and Victoria attended Jade Jagger's party the night before a game...

Leather together! David and Victoria wow onlookers yet again with their fashion statements...

from the stands as Manchester United fought out a close game that was eventually won by a single goal from Andy Cole. Observers who imagined that the reluctant spectator would have drawn some measure of satisfaction from anything other than a Man Utd victory know nothing of the fire that drives David Beckham. He wants desperately to play in every game and finds watching from the stands as frustrating as most professionals. But more than anything else he is dedicated to making Manchester United the most successful team in the land.

⚽ David is not one of those footballers who rate the pleasure more highly than sex: 'I'm often asked the question which is better and for me there is no question. Of course sex is better.'

After watching an early screening in Manchester of the British movie Bend It Like Beckham about a women's football team, David and Victoria liked the film so much that they asked if they could play themselves in the finished version. They entered into negotiations to play themselves in the final sequence but in the end lookalikes were used when the couple could not find the time to film their scenes. The movie gets its title from David's ability to bend the ball into the goalmouth. The movie stars former All Saint singer Shaznay Lewis, Juliet Stevenson, and Keira Knightley who said after being put through ten weeks of intensive football training: 'Now I fully realise how absolutely brilliant a footballer Beckham is.'

One of the many fine qualities of Alex Ferguson as a manager is that he does not bear grudges. Once he has delivered his point of view, however blistering, he is prepared to move on for the good of the team. The Leeds incident was not allowed to spoil the relationship between manager and star.

Less seriously, David once went to a party given by Jade Jagger in London the night before the team was due to fly out to Austria to play a European Champions League fixture against Sturm Gratz. Jade was a friend and David and Victoria wanted to support her, but their appearance led to desperately exaggerated newspaper stories about the footballer being out on the town late at night. In fact he left the party early and typically drank nothing alcoholic while he was there. But it was the wrong sort of publicity and David was quick to apologise to the manager.

The most trivial incident can be publicised out of all proportion when David Beckham is involved, and that feeds the gossip that forever follows England's football hero. News that David and Victoria were a few minutes late for Alex Ferguson's testimonial dinner in Manchester was reported as if it made for a major international incident. In fact the couple were delayed, like countless parents before them, by trying to settle Brooklyn down for his babysitter. David shrugs off the ever-present irritation of inaccurate stories as an inevitable consequence of his success on the pitch. But that does not mean that it does not get under his skin.

The situation is exacerbated by the fact that David has to deal with a great deal of false information about his life. Alex

Ferguson rang him up one afternoon just as he was heading off for a sauna in Manchester and asked where he was. David explained and his manager replied: 'Oh right. I have just had a call to say someone is sitting next to you at Barcelona Airport.'

David is immensely proud to play for Manchester United. 'You have got to have a certain amount of arrogance to play at Manchester United,' he admits. 'It is such a big club with so many expectations of you as a player. If you look through the United teams over the last 10 years they have had players who have got both the arrogance and the determination to win. That is pumped into us even at a young age. We have all got the aggression. It has been proved a number of times.

> 'I couldn't see myself playing for another club in this country, it has never crossed my mind. The thought of pulling on a shirt other than the red one of United just doesn't appeal to me.'
>
> (David Beckham)

We all stick together. That is the important thing.' (That said, although he loves scoring goals, David is not one of those footballers who rate the pleasure more highly than sex: 'I'm often asked the question which is better and for there is no question. Of course sex is better. I can't keep my hands off Victoria, anyway!')

One of the great strengths of Manchester United is the bond between the team members. Not only are they exceptionally good players in their own right, but many of them are very close after playing together for many years. They instinctively know how the others will react to any

Eyebrows were raised at Old Trafford when Manchester United's most expensive signing, £23.5 million Argentinian midfield star Juan Sebastian Veron, arrived for medical checks in July 2001 and was photographed wearing the famous number seven shirt. There was some 'history' between the two players with Veron playing opposite Beckham in the 1998 World Cup game between England and Argentina in which David Beckham was controversially sent off. The famous number seven shirt – previous occupants have included George Best, Bryan Robson and Eric Cantona – is not something that David Beckham would ever give up lightly. But there was no need for David to get shirty. Manchester United announced quickly that it was all just a coincidence and Veron was just wearing a 'training shirt'.

given situation and they all work very hard for each other on the pitch. 'That is the good thing about our team,' David explains. 'You don't get players hiding during a game. Players work hard not just for themselves but for the team. If you look around the team every player works for each other. If one player goes forward another will step in. That was the work ethic we have had pumped into us ever since we were apprentices. Me, Gary Neville, Phil Neville, Paul Scholes, Nicky Butt and Ryan Giggs were all brought up to work hard at our game and we knew the rewards in front of us if we did. We had to go back in the afternoons, and some

⚽ 'Time is the one thing that is so precious,'

of us went back in the evenings, to work with the kids who were coming up when we were apprentices.'

And what of those rumours that circulate periodically, suggesting that David Beckham might be considering a move elsewhere? 'There is no other club I want to play for,' he maintains. 'I love playing in front of more than 60,000 people. I would not be able to get that anywhere else in the Premiership... There is no bigger club in the world so why

Brian Clough, who said of David: 'He should sign a new, long contract with United, persuade his missus to have a few more bairns and get as much rest as he can.

should I want to leave? I have said in the past that I might want to play abroad at some stage, but at the moment all I can see is turning out for United and helping them to be even more successful.'

Even during the most tense moments of his recent contract negotiations, David Beckham's determination to clinch a satisfactory deal has never affected his devotion to the club. 'I want to carry on playing for Manchester United,' he stated for the record. 'They're the team I support, they're the team my family support and it's the place where I'm most loved by the fans and I love them.'

David won Man Utd.com's Player Of The Season award for 2000/01, receiving more than quarter of the votes. More than 94,000 fans from all over the world voted in the poll by clicking on the official website's home page. David finished with 25.7 per cent of the votes.

Many fine players find a new lease of life in football as managers when their playing days are over. However, David Beckham has no such plans – he thinks it's just too stressful. At the same time that popular Liverpool manager Gerard Houllier was released from hospital after heart surgery, the England captain was telling the papers: 'I don't want to be a manager or a coach. I will have had stress and hassle for 20 years so it will be a relief. I would rather be involved with kids, developing talent in young players.'

David's one ambition is for a long time off once he gives up playing. (He has already decided that when he can no longer compete with the very best players he will hang up his boots for good. The idea of slipping slowly down the leagues as a shadow of his former self horrifies him.) He would love to take a year out, or perhaps even longer, to spend time with his family, perhaps switching the concentration to Victoria. 'Time is the one thing that is so precious,' he insists. 'It flashes past so quickly that you really should make sure you get the most out of your life. After I stop playing I want to take a long look at what to do with the rest of my life. But hopefully that is still a long time away. There are a lot of trophies to be won before then.'

Few would doubt he has the talent to win them. On the day Beckham was voted runner up to Real Madrid's Luis Figo as World Footballer Of The Year in 2001, West Ham's Paolo Di Canio commented: 'Beckham is the best player in the world at the moment. In the old days they said he could only cross a ball. But now he scores goals, he fights, he leads the team, he plays left, right, centre, everywhere. Fantastic. When you play at Old Trafford and his name is not on the team sheet, you are happy because you know if you give him a couple of free-kicks you will surely die.'

And if that's not praise enough, here's what outspoken former soccer manager Brian Clough has to say on the subject of David Beckham's future: 'Highly talented player who plays for the team and Alex Ferguson has done a brilliant job with him. When necessary he has cracked down on him and Beckham has juggled all the social balls well.' Interestingly, though, Clough also sounds a note of caution: 'But what happens when Alex retires? Will the glamour of Milan and Madrid get to him? When you're young, you can get away with all the whizzing around but it does catch up with you. He's a fit lad now, but if he stops doing his stuff on match day, all that magazine and TV documentary trivia will rebound on him. He should sign a new, long contract with United, persuade his missus to have a few more bairns and gets as much rest as he can.'

CHAPTER 3

POSH AND BECKS

David and Victoria at their first ever meeting.

DAVID BECKHAM and Victoria Adams have become one of the most popular celebrity couples in modern times. They are frequently compared to Richard Burton and Elizabeth Taylor at the height of their fame, but in fact Posh and Becks have filled more acres of newsprint than any other twosome. Yet it all started so casually. David first met the only non-blonde he had ever dated at a football match in London. He shyly acknowledged the presence of the Spice Girl who looked so much more beautiful in the flesh

⚽ **'I love Victoria for herself. I would love her even if she was working in Tesco's.'**

than he could have imagined, but it was left to her to start a proper conversation. (Victoria's pop star status did not impress David Beckham when they first met. He said: 'I love Victoria for herself. I would love her even if she was working in Tesco's.')

Let's get this straight from the start: David Beckham is a gentleman. One of the first things that Victoria Adams

The world gets its first glimpse of baby Brooklyn as David leaves the hospital with his new son.

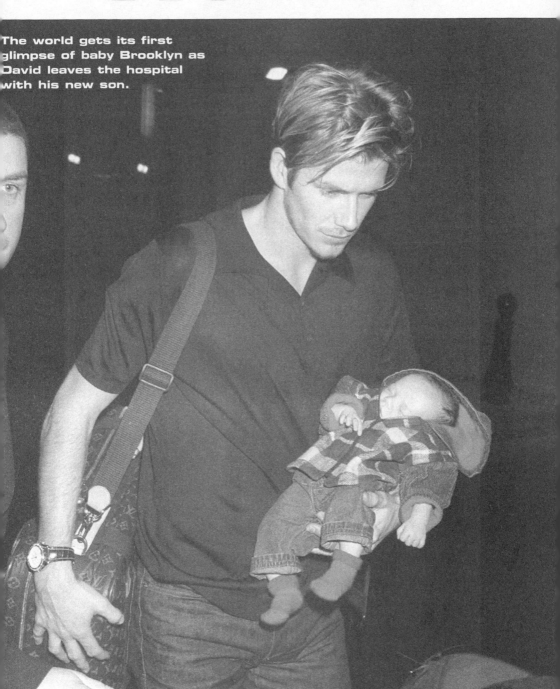

73

noticed about the behaviour of her future husband was that he stands up when a woman comes into the room. That is the way he was brought up, and if it seems old-fashioned he couldn't care less. Victoria thought it was wonderful. For his part, David was instantly attracted to Victoria but in spite of his apparent assurance he is very shy. He found it hard to show he was so taken with this confident young pop star who was every bit as successful in her field as he was in his. So it was left to Victoria to initiate the swapping of telephone numbers.

Gradually the young couple realised that the attraction was mutual. They knew they could not meet in a public place without being jointly mobbed so they arranged a meeting at the home of Victoria's fellow Spice Girl, Melanie C. David was delighted to learn that the Spice Girls were in their own way every bit as supportive a team as his fellow players at Manchester United. They wanted to be sure Posh Spice was not going to be messed around by a fly-by-night footballer. Naturally, that was never on the cards. David gradually won their trust and they all became firm friends.

> 'I knew as soon as I met him that one of the most attractive things about David was that he shared the same sort of family values as me. I really liked that.'
>
> Victoria Beckham

David is a self-confessed enthusiast of the mobile phone, and he and Victoria find it is a vital tool in ensuring they keep in touch with each other wherever their busy lives take them. Early on in their relationship, when Victoria was away touring, the mobile became David's vital only link to his lover and his monthly bills were astronomical. Manager Sir Alex Ferguson was concerned that his young star was not distracted from his game. Team-mate Brian McClair recalls that the boss was less than amused when one of his all-important pre-match team talks was interrupted by the sound of a mobile ringing. As Sir Alex was carefully assessing the strengths and weaknesses of the afternoon's opposition, 'David Beckham's mobile phone rang and he jumped miles into the air in his embarrassment,' McClair reveals. 'The manager did not bat an eyelid, merely took it off him and dropped it in the bin.'

David loves Victoria's confidence and her sparky sense of humour and she loves his warmth and quiet authority. Their initial encounter was as close to love at first sight as it gets in their highly charged world of telephone-number bank balances and towering egos. At the very basis of their relationship is trust. In professions hardly famous for encouraging fidelity, David and Victoria knew from the very start that it would be all or nothing for them. The opportunities for casual affairs in their high-speed worlds are always there but fortunately for both of them they met at a time when both were absolutely ready for total commitment. The constant touching and hand-holding is a genuine expression of their love for each other and they are both fully determined to stay together for life.

The couple had been seeing each other for around six

Victoria shows off her magnificent wedding ring as she and David announce their engagement.

months when David proposed, in traditional fashion. They had already talked in detail about their future life together and there was no doubt that Victoria was going to say 'Yes'. David cheerfully accepts the public perception that the more verbal and outgoing Victoria is seen as the dominant partner, but in fact neither member of the couple is the more assertive. David is very much in love with Victoria but they always make their decisions jointly and his softly spoken views are given just as much weight as her more forcefully voiced opinions. Friends note how much they have both matured since they have been together and the relationship is strong and healthy despite the unrelenting glare of the media spotlight.

But for David even more important than Victoria's agreement to marry him was the news that she was pregnant. Victoria was in the New York district of Brooklyn at the time – hence the name of their chirpy first son who has played such an enormous part in the development of a marked maturity in David. Baby Brooklyn Joseph Beckham was born just before eight o'clock on the morning of March 4, 1999. He weighed in at seven pounds; Victoria had a Caesarean birth with David and her mum by her side. Attention from press and public was so intense at the London hospital that they had a police escort all the way back to her parents' home in Hertfordshire. Bookmakers were instantly offering odds of 10,000 to one that Brooklyn would be one day sent off against Argentina! One of David and Victoria's first decisions was not to follow so many affluent and busy couples and hire a nanny. The Beckhams are determined to care for their son themselves and they prefer to rely on their mothers if they do need help. The idea of Brooklyn running to a nanny for comfort instead of to one of them horrifies both parents. To mark the importance of Brooklyn in his life, David had a tattoo of a male guardian angel put in place on his back. It was an extremely painful experience, but he felt it was well worth it. He also has a tattoo of Victoria's name spelled out in Hindi. He says he tried it out in Chinese first, copying the letters out with the help of the translation on the menu of the local take-away. 'It probably said "fried rice", instead of "Victoria!" he joked afterwards.

The strength of the emotions he experienced through becoming a father really surprised David Beckham. Footballers are not famous for their sensitivity but David was totally bowled over, first by the news that Victoria was pregnant, and even more so later by the birth of Brooklyn. He has since stated that that feeling of holding his son in his arms was the most moving moment of his life. All of a sudden a new life was there in his arms and it was more important than even the most crucial of football matches. Victoria pays tribute to her husband's dogged determination to be an attentive and caring father. She is certain it is one of the characteristics which makes him such a fantastic footballer: 'When he gets a bee in his bonnet he will do what he wants to do. David is a very deep and philosophical man.'

The second the couple became a family is one that David

David shows off the Hindi tattoo he had done in Victoria's honour. He copied the lettering off a chinese menu, and joked that it probably says 'fried rice'.

Beckham will treasure for the rest of his life. It gave him a new perspective on his other achievements, and a new responsibility. He responded by taking on as many baby caring duties as time would allow. He was not feeding his son and changing his nappy for publicity or to impress anyone else. He simply felt so instantly devoted to this warm and helpless new arrival that every moment away from him was hard to bear. He has told friends how he finds that he spends hours just staring at his young son. 'It feels like he is somehow a part of me,' he says. 'When I was little I can remember hurting my foot at football and it was really aching and my dad could see I was in a lot of pain. He said, "If I could have that pain in my leg, I would son." I didn't really think he meant it at the time. I thought it was just a nice thing for a dad to say. But

Victoria says that her song 'Every Little Part Of Me' is about 'how me and David made Brooklyn together.'

now I realise that he really did mean it. I would have all Brooklyn's pains if I could. I would do anything to make his life as good as possible and becoming a father has given me a fantastic new sense of purpose.'

David said that of course he will do everything he can to protect and look after Victoria. But he knows that she is a strong independent woman. There is something about babies, though. They are just so small and helpless and they need their parents to do everything for them. The jobs have always been a joy to David, he has enjoyed everything from the feeds to the nappy changing. And now, after the

David never shies away from being affectionate with Brooklyn in public.

announcement in early 2002 that Victoria is pregnant once more, he is looking forward to doing it all over again. David says he doesn't mind whether Victoria has another boy or a girl, just so long as it is healthy. And he wants to have a large and happy family.

David and Victoria are determined to bring up their son to be caring and polite. The first word Brooklyn learned was 'please'. Victoria says: 'I am going to be strict with him because I do like very well-behaved children. I am not going to let him run around in restaurants. People might say I am being stuck up and snobbish but it costs nothing to be polite. A lot of people have said, "Oh, Brooklyn's going to be a spoilt little boy." But I hate nasty children.' Brooklyn already likes to kick a ball and David wants to bring his son up to share his deep love of the game. 'There is nothing better than seeing kids enjoy playing football,' he insists.

The Beckhams are going to wait until Brooklyn is older before they make any big decisions on his religious upbringing. David revealed in September 2000 that he was one-quarter Jewish. He said his mother's father was Jewish and added: 'I have probably had more contact with

Judaism than any other religion. I used to wear skull caps when I was younger and I also went to some Jewish weddings with my grandfather.'

Posh and Becks's own wedding was planned like a military operation. It might have looked like a glitzy, expensive affair but in fact David and Victoria planned the

David and Victoria have reached the state of pseudo-royals – at their wedding they even had their own thrones!

whole day to give real meaning to their relationship with each other and with their families. They dispensed with the tradition of stag nights and hen parties, for a start. Neither of them wanted to celebrate their marriage starting with strippers and drunkenness so they opted instead for a family dinner and a quiet moment afterwards with their son. As a venue for their wedding, the couple chose romantic Luttrellstown Castle in Ireland, a huge ivy-clad fortress that had a tiny stone folly a few hundred yards from the main building which would be perfect for the ceremony. After some consideration, the couple decided to accept the offer of £1 million from *OK!* magazine for all the pictures of the big day. And it was not just the money that influenced that decision – by then David and Victoria were each wealthy enough in their own right to pay whatever it took. They just didn't have the time or the organisation to handle security. Press interest was at fever pitch in the run-up to the wedding. Even before the wedding invitations had been sent out, one was stolen and found its way to a newspaper.

But nothing could spoil the big day, not even poor Brooklyn throwing up over David's shirt! David and Victoria were married by the Bishop of Cork. The speeches were warm and moving and at some point or other just about everyone was in tears; David was anxious about making his own speech and he worked hard to get it just right. Elton John couldn't make because he was ill but the Spice Girls, minus the departed Geri Halliwell, were there.

The couple borrowed Sir Andrew Lloyd Webber's

All smiles
from David
and best man
Gary Neville.

fabulous house at Cap Ferrat in the South of France for their honeymoon – with Brooklyn, of course. However, they didn't have much time to enjoy each other's company, because David had to be back in Manchester for training.

The marriage is very important to both partners. They feel it has enriched and deepened their relationship. But David works hard to see that their life together is never boring. When he found he had a few free days in his normally busy schedule with Manchester United he went to great lengths to organise to take Victoria and Brooklyn away on a surprise trip to Tuscany, where they love to relax and spend some time away from the publicity spotlight. David took a lot of trouble to disguise his plans, even sending the luggage to the airport separately, so that he could enjoy the look of delight on his wife's face when he finally told her he was giving her what she most wants in life – time out with her husband and child. Victoria responded by surprising David with a flying one-day visit from both their mums on his birthday.

Ever the romantic, David sent Victoria a single yellow rose every day until they began living together. These days, if work commitments mean they have to be apart, he sends her two yellow roses. On their first anniversary, he organised a surprise Chinese take-away meal for Victoria by setting up a table with a crisp white tablecloth and two chairs on the roof of their Hertfordshire mansion where they dined by candlelight under the stars and toasted each other with champagne. And in the spring of 2001, he whisked her off on a surprise trip to Venice – she was under the impression they were going to Paris – and a romantic ride on a gondola.

Of course, when a super-rich, internationally famous husband and wife also happen to be sex symbols, they're bound to attract attention from certain quarters... David and Victoria were offered £100,000 each to pose naked together for *Playboy* magazine. They turned it down, but Victoria said later: 'I would seriously consider it in future. They have done tasteful poses in the past. We will just have to wait and see what happens. Who knows?'

> **'I don't wear her knickers. It would be a bit worrying if I did because she's a bit smaller than me.'**
>
> David Beckham

The Beckhams have certainly courted their fair share of controversy in their time. Victoria unwittingly created quite a stir in the media when she jokingly told Johnny Vaughan on TV that David wore her thong knickers – prompting Radio One DJ Chris Moyles to dedicate Sisqo's big chart hit 'Thong Song' to the Beckhams before England's game against Portugal. 'Victoria obviously says things now and again that makes it a little bit worse for me,' David later admitted to Michael Parkinson on his chat show. He went on: 'Victoria is always being asked who wears the trousers in the relationship. I can assure you that I am my own man, but we make the big decisions about our life together. What some people don't realise is that Victoria says a lot of things tongue-in-cheek. The comment about me wearing her knickers was a joke. Everyone should have known that. But for four or five days it was all people wanted to talk about. It was embarrassing and she shouldn't have said it, even in fun. But then we had a laugh about it. It didn't cause any trouble between us.'

'When Victoria starts talking, sometimes she can't stop,' he added. 'She says things that get a bit of coverage but I love her still so it doesn't matter.' Both Beckhams are super-successful although David says that his wife Victoria makes more money than him. 'She has a go at me sometimes for my spending,' he admits, 'but she knows it's mine, well ours, and if I want something I'll get it, within reason. Maybe sometimes I am flash but at the end of the day if I'm happy and can afford it I don't see a problem.' The couple were adamant that they didn't want a pre-nuptial agreement to take care of their different-sized fortunes in case of any split. 'It starts off marriage on the wrong foot,' said David. 'We put our money into a joint account. That was the first sort of concrete thing between us, the joint account. Everything goes in there.'

> 'She earns more than me. That's why I married her, for her money.'
>
> David Beckham

Of course, when you're in the Beckhams' league it's only natural to want to spend some of your millions on the odd indulgence. David loves jewellery and he can afford the best. Among his most prized possessions is a glittering £50,000 Franck Muller watch. It goes with his diamond and gold wedding band, worth the same amount, that Victoria bought for her husband from the stylish boutique at Place Vendôme in Paris. David loves wonderful watches and top-quality jewellery and among his favourite gifts from Victoria are his £5,000 diamond cross earrings for his 26th birthday in May 2001 and his £15,000 Van Cleef and Arpels engagement ring, which she bought in Beverly Hills. He loves to give as well as to receive. Among the elegant gifts he has bought for his wife is a beautiful Boodle & Dunthorne marquise-cut diamond engagement ring, which cost £40,000, and a gold, diamond-studded bracelet from Cartier, which cost around £10,000.

Unfortunately, despite – or perhaps because of – their success, the Beckhams have come in for more than their fair share of criticism as a couple. Colourful Manchester socialite and club owner Frank 'Foo Foo' Lammar is a close friend of David and Victoria and he is furious at the way they are constantly misrepresented in the press. 'Without doubt David and Victoria are the most recognised and glamorous couple in the country,' he says, 'and rarely a day passes without, for one reason or another, one or both of them appearing in the national press. And yet a lot of these stories are total fabrication, or to put it another way, complete rubbish. Let me give you an example. People who know me are well aware of the charity work I do and David and Victoria are always willing to help me – for no personal gain or recognition – at short notice and whenever their busy work commitments allow. They are

**Frank 'Foo Foo' Lamarr, Manchester
entertainer and close friend of David and Victoria.**

regular visitors with me to various hospitals where they will
spend time donating and handing out presents to sick
children and signing countless autographs. I can assure you
they do this completely from the heart and not for any
personal publicity. Indeed the majority of these visits
attracts no press coverage whatsoever and this is the way
they want it to be.

'One particular story in the press told of the couple

supposedly "cruising" around Cheshire in their new Ferrari and shopping for baby clothes. I knew this was a completely fictitious story as they were with me for most of the day visiting a hospital. I felt so strongly about this that I even wrote a letter to the paper concerned expressing my disgust, going on to say that they never seem to write about the good in people, only the apparent bad.

'Many times I have seen children's faces light up when I have arrived in their wards with my two special friends,' he continues. 'Doctors tell me regularly that whatever medicine they can administer pales into insignificance compared with the effects of a visit from the Beckhams. A lot of things said and written about David and Victoria Beckham are just pure envy. So what if they can afford to go shopping in a Ferrari, anyway? They didn't start out in this life with a Ferrari – they've earned it, and wouldn't you go shopping in a Ferrari if you had one? David and Victoria Beckham are genuine people and first-class humanitarians.'

There are plenty of examples that back up Frank's generous praise of Posh and Becks. Seven-year-old Dean Cooper from Bramall, who had spent much of his young life in hospital fighting a series of cruel blood disorders, was asleep in Royal Manchester Children's Hospital when two very famous visitors arrived to see him. David and Victoria Beckham stood for several moments looking down at the gravely ill youngster, who was oblivious of their presence. A kindly nurse stepped in to tell them, 'We'll have to wake him. He'll never forgive us if he misses you.' So Dean was gently nudged awake and his eyes widened in astonishment as he saw his favourite footballer looking down at him. He was speechless. His bedroom walls at home were covered with posters of David Beckham, but seeing the real thing at his bedside was clearly just too much for him. He rubbed the sleep from his eyes and Victoria leaned forward and said, 'Sorry to wake you up, Dean. David and I just wanted to say we hope you get better soon.' The beam of delight that spread across Dean's face threatened to light up the whole ward. David sat down on the hospital bed and chatted quietly to Dean about Manchester United's title chances and his famous long-distance goal against Wimbledon. Afterwards, Dean's father Dennis Cooper said: 'I'm not ashamed to say I cried my eyes out afterwards. Poor Dean has not had a lot to smile about for a long time, but he absolutely idolises David Beckham. For him to get a personal visit and a long one-to-one chat was just the best present you

> **'They make everyone feel good and I honestly believe that it gives a genuine medical boost in some cases.'**
>
> A consultant at Rachel's hospital

could give him. David was wonderful. He told Dean that you have to keep fighting to get better and he chatted to him about Ryan Giggs and Paul Scholes. Dean has not stopped smiling since. There were no photographers and no publicity and David and Victoria spent hours talking to kids. I'd like to thank them both with all my heart for the wonderful lift they gave my son.'

David receives a peck on the cheek from one of his many admirers!

David and Victoria Beckham gave 16-year-old leukaemia victim Lauren Bradley a wonderful Christmas lift when they made a surprise visit to see her in hospital. Lauren simply worships David and she was one of many youngsters cheered up by the caring Beckhams in a visit to the Christie Hospital in Manchester that – once again – the couple were anxious to keep secret. 'They asked me how I was and if I was a Manchester United fan,' said Lauren. 'I am a fan, particularly of David. They seemed really nice and down to earth.' David and Victoria made the visit after other Manchester United players had told them how disappointed the children were that they were not able to take part in a previous visit.

On another occasion, David spent time with seven-year-old Rachel Heys, from Kirkham near Blackpool, who has a rare soft tissue cancer. 'David sat with me and even gave me a kiss,' Rachel revealed, an act that her mum described as 'a lovely warm gesture'. 'The impact of these sort of visits is astonishing,' a consultant at Rachel's hospital explained. 'It can be a pretty difficult business being ill and the routine of a busy hospital means the staff don't have as much time as they would like to keep the patients' spirits up. A popular couple like David and Victoria can do enormous good with a visit like this... I have never seen a football match in my life and I certainly do not listen to pop music but David and Victoria can certainly add me to their long list of fans.'

When David led England out on to the field at Old Trafford against Greece in 2002, he was clutching the hand of Kirsty Howard, a six-year-old girl who was suffering from an inoperable heart condition. 'She inspired the whole England team when she went on to the pitch holding David's hand,' Victoria remembered. 'There are not many young ladies that I let hold hands with my husband, but I know she has a special place in his heart.' Six months later Victoria met up with Kirsty again in

London when she opened the Harrods February sale and helped appeal for funds to help the Francis House Hospice in Manchester, which helped care for Kirsty.

BECKINGHAM PALACE

Sleepy Sawbridgeworth has never been quite the same since David Beckham and his wife Victoria moved into their magnificent £4 million mansion, which is set in 24 acres right on the Essex-Hertfordshire border. (One of the big selling points about the lovely house was that it is very close to Victoria's parents' home in Goff's Oak,

The Beckhams' magnificent home in Sawbridgeworth.

Hertfordshire.) The house had once been a home for disabled children, but had subsequently fallen into disrepair and the previous owner had renovated the place before selling on to the Beckhams in 1999. It has seven bedrooms, an indoor swimming pool and now has a recording studio, a bathroom dedicated to Victoria's idol Audrey Hepburn, a snooker room, a gym and state-of-the-art, floodlit tennis courts.

The locals mostly welcomed the young couple with open arms. The only person reported not to be too pleased with the arrival was the other local celebrity – Dame Barbara Cartland. She said the town would be better off without the Beckhams and sneered that they had: 'Lots of money but no class.'

The former owner had created a French chateau-style interior, which was swiftly removed. The Beckhams clearly had their own ideas about interior decoration – particularly Victoria. 'It is an old house and I have themed every room,' the former Spice Girl once explained. 'It's really camp. There is a room like a tart's boudoir with leopard-print everywhere and a mirrored ceiling. Then there is our bedroom, which is quite virginal and white, with a big four-poster, old oak bed. The hall has bright red walls, a huge tacky chandelier and big thick velvet curtains.' Brooklyn's bedroom has hundreds of fibre-optic lights set in the ceiling to recreate the night sky. Before long, the house had been dubbed Beckingham Palace. (In keeping with the theme of bold-as-you-like interior decoration, a huge photograph of David

and Victoria kissing dominates their luxurious penthouse flat in Manchester, which has been carefully designed with flamboyant leopard-print furnishings throughout.)

Well, most people who lived nearby could not have agreed less. Hairdresser Greg Rattey welcomed the couple with open arms. Already a Spice girls fan, he and his staff dressed up as the group for their 1997 Christmas party. Greg was even hopeful that David and Victoria would pop into his salon for a trim. He announced that it would be

£12 for David and £25 for Victoria. 'They could both have a wash and blow dry for that,' he explained. 'And I would do a very nice job. At the prices they normally pay, I reckon it has to be a bargain. I am a huge David Beckham fan. He is gorgeous.'

Staff at the Peking Palace Chinese restaurant advised David and Victoria to book early if they fancied a meal there. 'On a Friday and Saturday it gets very busy. But we could deliver a meal for two for £19.' At the off-licence the assistants were very excited when David called to stock up on drink. Alex Head served David and noted: 'He came in here and some boy dropped a bottle of beer in surprise when he turned round and suddenly saw the England football captain. He spent just over £200. He bought beer, wine, spirits and a couple of bottles of champagne.'

Tommy Barnet, landlord of The Gate, David Beckham's local Sawbridgeworth pub, quipped: 'David Beckham wouldn't get in my pub side – he's not good enough. But the real reason is that the man who plays in Beckham's position is my son Gary. And, as we all know, blood is thicker than water. But if David can get up on a Sunday, we'll give him a run out and see what he's like.' Tommy, who played for Crystal Palace in the Sixties, for Romford in the old Southern League, and was formerly chairman of Essex League team Sawbridgeworth FC, adds: 'I was a bit upset when David Beckham moved into the area. Till then I was the only football legend round here! But, seriously, we've seen him about the town and he comes across very well. He's done a hell of a lot for the town. He's put Sawbridgeworth on the map. You don't have to say where Sawbridgeworth is now. People say: "That's where David Beckham lives."'

And Tommy has no doubts that the arrival of a worldwide football legend has benefited the local area. 'He's good for the community in lots of ways,' he explains. 'He gave two signed shirts to help raise money for a local cerebral palsy cause. He's a very, very charitable guy. He's top of the pole in my estimation. David's welcome in my pub any time, even though I'm an Arsenal supporter.'

David was very concerned about security and privacy at the couple's new house, but his plans to build a 2.5-metre high brick wall round their luxurious property were thwarted by the planning authorities, who decided it was 'inappropriate and not in keeping with the village'. (A scaled-down version was accepted.)

*   *   *

A while back, David and Victoria gave an interview to *OK!* magazine that spelled out the strength of their feelings for each other in no uncertain terms. 'I really love David,' Victoria stated for the record. 'We are both very, very affectionate to each other. I have never been like this with any other boyfriends. I knew from early on how strongly I felt.' David agreed: 'I was the same. It was that feeling you have of wanting to be with someone, of wanting to make the effort to go and see them. I had never had that before.

There is trust between us as well, and as long as that is there then it will always be the relationship it is. The fact is, this is the first time I have been in love. Once you meet the person that you want to spend the rest of your life with, you dedicate your life to that person. You would never hurt or destroy that relationship.'

No doubt about it, as far as Posh and Becks are concerned, life's a family affair, right down the line. David even secretly sang backing vocals on Victoria's debut solo single 'Out Of Your Mind'. 'You can't really hear him at first,' Victoria admitted afterwards, 'but if you concentrate, you can hear him singing along with Dane Bowers who recorded with me. David has always wanted to sing along on a record so Dane and I thought it would be a bit of fun. We all had a great time working on the track. It's been a great family effort.'

CHAPTER 4

ENGLAND STAR

IN 1997, George Best was chosen as the top British player of all-time in a worldwide poll, and used the occasion to suggest David Beckham was the one man who could win the World Cup for England. The year before France '98, George said: 'If I were Glenn Hoddle in the few months left before the World Cup I would tell Beckham, "You are the boss. Go out and do it." Give him the captaincy, give him the centre of midfield, give him the authority, give him whatever it takes. You win the big prizes only if you have a main man who can be your winner.

'When you look back over past World Cups, the main man has always been the hub of the team,' George pointed out. 'Look at Pele, Beckenbauer, Cruyff and Eusebio. If this kid decides he wants to do it, he has the ability. What he still lacks is the final knife, the final killing off of opponents, but he is very close to it. I think so highly of Beckham that I believe he could become the Eric Cantona of Manchester United and he could reach similar heights for England.'

**Another famous wearer of the Number 7 shirt –
George Best.**

David Beckham received his first England call-up when the national team were being managed by Glenn Hoddle. In his own playing days, Hoddle had a flair for making decisive long and accurate passes that frequently changed the course of a game. As a schoolboy, David had greatly admired the cool elegance of the Hoddle game and the admiration was evidently mutual. Hoddle selected a 21-year-old David for his full England debut in the World Cup qualifying game against Moldova in September 1996. David put in a fine performance and held his place in the side throughout the whole round of qualifying matches that eventually saw England stake a place in France '98.

It was with high hopes and excitement that David Beckham joined the England squad at the golf resort in La Manga, Spain for the World Cup finals. He was delighted to be included in Hoddle's squad, but a little down that his close friends Nicky Butt and Phil Neville did not make the line-up. There was great controversy when Hoddle decided to dispense with the services of Paul Gascoigne: senior players started to question the way Gazza had been treated and suggested that this was hardly the best preparation for the World Cup. But as the tournament approached, David Beckham had his own problems to deal with after the manager decided to leave him out of the first match against Tunisia in Marseilles. Hoddle went on to explain that he did not consider that David was focused on the competition, and picked Darren Anderton in his place. To make matters worse, the bitterly disappointed youngster was presented to a press conference full of journalists anxious to make column inches on his feelings about being dropped. (That said, David was the only player to start every one of England's World Cup 1998 qualifying games under Glen Hoddle.) It was a real trial of his resolve, as he was forced to watch England beat Tunisia 2-0 with goals from Alan Shearer and Paul Scholes.

David finally joined the action when he was brought on as substitute in the game against Romania after Paul Ince was injured. It looked as if England

⚽ **That said, David was the only player to start every one of England's World Cup 1998 qualifying games under Glenn Hoddle.**

were going to snatch a draw when Michael Owen equalised towards the end but a last-minute winner gave the Romanians a 2-1 victory. England now had to beat Colombia in the last group game and David chose just the right moment to score his first goal for his country – a spectacular goal from a free-kick that curled at pace into the top corner and helped England win 2-0.

That goal helped put England through to a quarter-final match against Argentina – and the incident that made Beckham the most talked-about man in England…

THAT RED CARD

Without doubt, the lowest point in David Beckham's career was when he was sent off playing for England against Argentina in the World Cup on June 30, 1998. A penalty each saw the well-balanced sides standing level at 1-1. David then put Michael Owen through with a neat pass for the

David lies on the floor having just kicked out at Simeone - a few seconds that dashed England's world cup hopes.

That red card.

young Liverpool striker to race through and score one of the finest world Cup goals of all time. But Argentina levelled and with the score at 2-2, David Beckham suddenly found himself making news for all the wrong reasons. Beckham's mad moment came in the second half of the match when Diego Simeone sent him sprawling with a rough tackle from behind. While Beckham was lying prone on the turf, Simeone stooped to ruffle his hair. This seemed to aggravate the young English star and, while still prone on the turf, he kicked out at the Argentinian player, who then – rather theatrically – fell over backwards. Simeone was given a yellow card by the referee Kim Milton Nielsen for his foul on Beckham. But the ref then pulled out a red card and sent Beckham off for his retaliatory kick.

England team-mate Darren Anderton: 'Becks went to chest it and it was a dreadful tackle on him. Becks got studded in the back. Then there were a few players around the referee, Batistuta again, with the old, "He should be booked, sent off," trying to provoke trouble.'

Peter Taylor, who later made Beckham England captain when he took temporary charge of the national team, commented: 'Simeone absolutely whacked David from behind and then actually tapped David on the head. I can't see how the referee saw all that and didn't punish Simeone.'

Referee Kim Milton Nielsen explained his controversial decision afterwards to the press: 'Even if Beckham hadn't hit him, it was violent conduct,' he insisted. 'The law says an attempt to kick a player, or kicking a player, is the same. For both situations, it's a red card. There's no discussion about that. I don't enjoy to send a player off. He was maybe, in his mind, very angry for the free-kick. I think in the same second he's done it, he's said: "Oh no!"'

And what of Diego Simeone, the man whose dramatic reaction to Beckham's flick of the foot saw one of England's brightest footballing hopes sent off, leaving his team one man down? 'These reactions are, in the referee's opinion, done with the intention of doing harm. But in reality he didn't do anything,' he admitted. 'I think he could have had a yellow card and that would have been enough. I went for the ball, couldn't get it and obviously fouled him. I fell on him and when he was getting up he reacted. These reactions tend to happen because of all the strong emotions and feeling in the game. I am moving backwards and he gives me a slight blow, which makes me lose my balance and fall. I think he could have had a yellow card and that would have been enough.'

> **'Wait a minute, he's taking another card out for David Beckham. It's a red card for David Beckham! Oh no!'**
> ITV commentator Brian Moore

England fan Malcolm Cowie injects a welcome sense of perspective on David Beckham's presence that night: 'People remember that game for three reasons – [for] Beckham's sending off, for England losing on a penalty shoot-out, and for Michael Owen's wonderful goal. Beckham got a lot of stick, but does anyone remember who provided that perfect pass up to Michael Owen for Owen to set off on that electrifying run which ended in an unforgettable goal? It was Beckham.'

England lost the game on penalties and there were plenty

of armchair critics who were quick to blame the whole of England's World Cup failure on David Beckham. The man himself cried bitterly after his sending off. He was absolutely devastated at England's exit from the 1998 World Cup.

After such an unexpected and hurtful end to his hopes for glory, David was determined to get to New York to be with Victoria as soon as possible. She had told him she was pregnant, though his elation at the news was clouded by his despair at being sent off in that crucial match. He flew back on one Concorde with the rest of the England team and wasted little time at Heathrow boarding another one heading for the States.

It seemed the whole country had something to say about that red card. Many were slow to forgive, wrongly arguing that David Beckham's moment of madness had cost England victory that night. Tony Banks, who was Sports Minister at the time, was scathing about the way Beckham was pilloried after being sent off during that vital World Cup game. 'The treatment of David Beckham was quite unacceptable, to be perfectly honest,' he insisted. 'He's a young man, he's very skilled, yes he throws the odd tantrum, but then, you know, you would expect that to happen. He's a young man and he's going to have to learn. But it's unfair to have treated him, in my opinion, in the way he has been treated – as some sort of pariah who personally, individually,

> 'People blamed Beckham for the defeat. I disagree. England lost because they should have had it sewn up during those excellent 20 minutes, but they didn't know how to do it.'
>
> Diego Simeone

Ray Wilkins, ex-Manchester United star who was also once sent off while playing for England: 'Getting sent off at any time is not the most pleasant occasion. But to get sent off in a World Cup, you do feel the lowest of the low. You feel you've let everybody down, your team mates, your country, your family, the lot. I can imagine how David would have been feeling that night against the Argentinians.'

was responsible for our exit from the World Cup. That is absolute nonsense, and anyone who knows anything about football knows that it's nonsense.'

Following David's World Cup sending off, fellow England star Gareth Southgate, a former public enemy number one after his penalty miss against Germany in Euro '96, advised him: 'Face up to your critics. The next few weeks are not going to be very nice. The poor lad has already gone through far more than I ever suffered,' Southgate admitted, 'but I can still give him some good advice because of my

'I was one of the substitutes on the bench and as he kicked out I said, "He's off." The ref nearly ruined his life.'

Paul Merson

own experience. I took a lot of stick, including verbal abuse, nasty letters and people crossing the street to avoid me. The way you deal with it is the important thing and I was determined to stand up, be a man and try to explain to all those critics that football is merely a game.' It must have

been gratifying for David to hear of a fellow professional's high opinion of his character: 'I have every confidence he can win this battle,' Southgate insisted, 'even though it is going to be hard for him. David seems a quiet lad, yet I have no doubt he possesses the character and personality to come through safely on the other side. He wouldn't have progressed as far he has in the game without a lot of inner strength.'

> **'According to the Argentine players it was the worst kick they had ever seen, and according to the English players it was nothing.'**
>
> Ref Kim Milton Nielsen

Amidst all the shouting, it was refreshing to hear voices arguing for a more conciliatory stance. The Bible Society, with the backing of the Archbishop of Canterbury, Dr George Carey, called on the nation to forgive David for being sent off. It issued its 'Call to forgive David Beckham' through its Open Book Project, which aims to apply the Bible to everyday life. Dr David Spriggs, Baptist minister

> **'I can't believe he sent him off for what was an innocuous little flick.'**
>
> Gary Lineker

and Director of The Bible Society said: 'David Beckham is a human being, like you and me. Every day, all of us make terrible mistakes, in our homes and families, at our places of work, and in our local communities. Sometimes our actions make David's mistake look very trivial. What is so important is that David has faced up to his mistake, and asked the forgiveness of his team-mates and the whole nation. This takes courage and should not be thrown back in his face. What is more, he has done precisely what the Bible calls everyone to do in such circumstances. If we don't forgive him now, we are guilty of terrible hypocrisy.'

⚽ **'David has faced up to his mistake, and asked the forgiveness of his team-mates and the whole nation.'**

Undoubtedly, the period after France '98 was a tough time for the Manchester United star, but his strong support from his family and his club got him through it. Alex Ferguson stood up for his player, criticising Glenn Hoddle for his handling of the situation. After the sad end to his World Cup hopes, David Beckham returned to Old Trafford determined to look forward and not backwards. The Manchester United boss was already unhappy with some aspects of the way his star player had been treated in the World Cup and he advised David that the match was already in the past and that he should put it behind him. Alex Ferguson was shrewdly supportive of his gifted midfielder and he cleverly coaxed the very best form out of the player who received merciless stick from fans at every away ground he visited. The fact that he returned the compliment with stunning displays throughout the season says a great deal for the Beckham character.

It was a desperately difficult time for young David. His family received abusive phone calls. He was widely criticised in the press. And for a time he was treated like a national outcast. When the new season started he found the aggro about his sending off followed him around for a while. At one match, top referee David Elleray was so horrified by the foul chants from West Ham fans – shouting obscenities about Victoria – that he stepped in to speak to the player. 'I had a few quiet words,' Elleray remembers. 'I told David that as a referee I was used to getting stick, and that he should just ignore it. I wanted to make sure that the things they were chanting didn't make David do anything he would later regret. There was no problem with David. He smiled and got on with the game. Referees can help players in these situations.'

David found the personal abuse upsetting but he was much more angry about those revolting songs about his wife – and even, with an unbelievably chilling cruelty, about the health of his baby son. It is hard to understand the mentality of the sort of so-called fans who will cheerfully chant filth about a baby. West Ham footballer Steve Lomas urged home supporters not to have a go at the local boy-turned-Manchester United star, as he felt the insults would probably only improve his performance. 'Don't pick on him or it might rebound on us,' Steve pleaded with his fellow Hammers fans. 'Ian Wright has already told me he loves being barracked by opposing supporters. It fires him up and puts an extra edge on his game. I suspect Beckham reacts the same way. We don't see him running round plotting revenge because of some senseless abuse he received from our supporters.'

When he returned to start the new season, David's team-mates and the manager seemed extra supportive. But he decided to keep his head down and do what he does best – play football. As Manchester United clicked into impressive treble-winning form, David Beckham was performing well right at the nerve centre of a wonderful football team.

Fraser Massey, a West Ham season ticket holder with a seat in the second row of the East Stand known as 'The Chicken Run', recalls: 'Manchester United came to Upton Park to play West Ham in what was Beckham's first game since being sent off against Argentina. In the days running up to the game, it became clear that he was going to get a lot of verbal flak from the crowd who were not going to let him forget about his sending off in the World Cup. Beckham was loudly booed every time he got the ball and was subjected to verbal abuse throughout the game. But it has to be said that he took it very well. Once, when the ball went out of play in front of the West Ham fans in the Chicken Run, he came over to pick up the ball to take the throw-in amidst a torrent of booing and caught my eye and actually winked at me!'

Gradually the memories of the sending off dimmed and David allowed himself a little more media exposure. An appearance on Parkinson showed the appealing side of David's personality and helped to change the mood of public disapproval.

The perceptive Michael Parkinson was quick to realise the enormous pressure that David Beckham and his family were subjected to from so-called football fans. Parkinson's earlier footballing hero was that other wonderfully gifted Manchester United player George Best, who was subjected to massive attention and publicity thanks to his sensational soccer skills and glamorous life off the field. But while George Best was often jeered by opposition fans perhaps the worst abuse he received was the tuneful song from Liverpool's Kop which sneered: 'Georgie Best, superstar, walks like a woman and he wears a bra.' George Best was well able to laugh that one off. But David Beckham is faced with fans screaming that they hope his young son dies of cancer or that his wife enjoys anal sex.

Parkinson was appalled by this vile treatment which he felt was a sad sign of the times we live in and also an illustration of plain jealousy. Some fans seemed to find it impossible to accept that one man could be so sublimely talented on the field and so blessed with his life away from football. Parkinson was mightily impressed by David Beckham's dignity as well as his skill. The highly respected writer and broadcaster was outraged that England's captain should have

⚽ **'Ferguson nursed the talent; Sven Goran Eriksson might be the man to grant it full expression.'**

to deal with this sort of level of unspeakable abuse. A silent majority of football supporters around the country must have quietly cheered Parkinson for pointing out the inspirational impact of David Beckham, which shows that even today it is possible to have a loving marriage, a happy family, and still become a national hero. David Beckham was grateful for Michael Parkinson's articulate support. They both knew that abuse from the terraces was never going deflect the player from striving towards his dream. As Parkinson said: 'Ferguson nursed the talent; Sven Goran Eriksson might be the man to grant it full expression.' And

Michael Parkinson,
one of David's
greatest admirers.

The face of football. David models the new Umbro England kit.

From boy to man. In a few short years, David has gone from being a fresh-faced teenager

to one of the most recognisable icons of modern times.

David displays the footballing skills against Luxembourg which have already made him a legend of the game.

David is well used to holding aloft silverware! Here he celebrates Manchester United's victory in the FA Carling Premiership.

Manchester United vs Bradford City.

David at the launch of his bestselling autobiography.

Whilst David is a sports icon on the pitch, he is a fashion icon off the pitch.
He is pictured here at the Sports Awards.

George Best certainly recognised that the man who now wears his famous shirt is a special talent, as he displayed when he installed David Beckham in his team of Man Utd greats.

Many decent football fans were already disgusted by the foul torrent of abuse David was subjected to and he was delighted that messages of personal support were starting to grow in number. When stand-in England manager Peter Taylor made David Beckham captain for a match against Italy on November 15, 2000, it sealed a total turnaround in the footballer's public image. The bad boy of St Etienne was, it seemed, not really so bad after all. And, in retrospect, no one player could genuinely have been held responsible for England's failure to progress further in the World Cup. David's tremendous form on the pitch helped inspire a new wave of warmth and popularity for the player. The fans could see how he responded to the challenge of becoming the nation's captain and they liked it. It had not been easy to make the journey from villain to hero, but David Beckham was delighted to have finally made the trip.

ENGLAND CAPTAIN

The first time David captained England on home soil was against Spain at Villa Park in a friendly on February 28, 2001. It was Sven Goran Eriksson's first England team and England won 3-0 on the day. Since then, Beckham has made the captain's armband his own. Former England skipper Terry Butcher really rates David Beckham as the leader of the national side: 'David Beckham is the first name I'd put down as England captain. He's not scratched the surface in terms of international football yet but I believe he can. He has played well under Sven Goran Eriksson and is the right charismatic character England need to lead the team. His biggest contribution at the moment will be as a player, let alone as captain.'

⚽ **'There's a new authority in my game, and that is something I needed to have in this job...'**

David Beckham himself took time to settle into the captain's role before grasping the appointment with both hands. He first said he did not consider he was a natural leader but later qualified his statement: 'When I said I wasn't a natural leader it was because I had never done the job and I thought it might take a while for me to get into it,' he explained. 'I believed I could do a decent job, but I knew I would have to work hard at it if I was going to succeed. I put in the work, and I believe I'm getting stronger as a captain all the time.

'I'm great deal more comfortable with being England captain,' he continued. 'There's a new authority in my game, and that is something I needed to have in this job… This is a new era, and one that has started well for the new

> **'To be captain of an England team at this point in time when we are doing so well is just one of the best honours I could ever have been given in football. When I had the phone call early in the morning from Peter Taylor to tell me I was captain, it took a minute to actually sink in'**
>
> David Beckham, on being made England captain

Sven Goran Eriksson – the man who seems to be taking David's talent to a different level.

England coach. To win his first three games and get six points from the two World Cup qualifying games must be brilliant for him, but then we will all be going home happy. We had set our sights on being on the seven-point mark in the group after these two games and we have done that. We are beginning to play some excellent football and the spirit in the dressing room is superb.

'The dream for me, for all of us, is to get to the World Cup. It was special three years ago, but to go there with this group of players would be wonderful. In players like Michael Owen we have the talent to get us there. He had one chance against Albania and he took it, though we knew if we carried on playing our football we would eventually break them down. We never resorted to hoofing the ball up the pitch.' (Talking of Owen, Beckham had the unusual experience of being cheered to the echo at Anfield, home of Manchester United's deadly rivals, when he scored the winner in England's 2-1 victory over Finland in a World Cup qualifying game on March 24, 2001.)

England manager Sven Goran Eriksson is a great admirer of David Beckham: 'It is difficult to find a better passer in the world today than David Beckham,' he says. 'I had two excellent passers at Lazio, in Veron and Mihajlovic, and if Beckham is not better than them he is certainly on the same level. In the games since I have come here, Beckham has done extremely well. He's hard working, a good passer, scores goals. I have absolutely no intention of changing captains; he is doing well, playing well and behaving well. Life cannot be easy for him always. He is one of the best players in the world, captain of England, playing for Manchester United and has a very famous wife, so whatever they do, it is, "click", photos all over the world. It is not a normal life.'

'Roy Keane is a fantastic skipper but I would love to succeed him eventually.'

David Beckham

No doubt about it, David loves captaining England – though needless to say, one day he would love to be captain of Manchester United as well. Right now, of course, that role is in the more than capable hands of Roy Keane.

David may be the most widely known England star in the

world right now, but he was upstaged by an unlikely character when England played Albania in the World Cup qualifiers: Norman Wisdom! The 86-year-old comic turned up to support the team and as a reflection of his unlikely popularity in Albania, which was brought

> 'There is a great belief in this squad, and everyone is excited about the future.'
>
> David Beckham

about by dictator Enver Hoxha. The now deposed leader banned most other western films during his reign apart from the ones featuring Norman playing hapless errand boy Norman Pitkin – he considered them a classic portrayal of an oppressed proletarian worker triumphing against overwhelming capitalist odds. 'I just thought they were funny,' said Norman. 'But I'm

> 'When he plays for Man U, I hate him. For England, I love him. But, above all as a footballer, for his commitment and work-rate, I respect him. I think that attitude towards Beckham from the Anfield crowd really came across when he scored there for England against Finland.'
>
> Liverpool fan Elliott Havakuk

over here to help. I think David Beckham is a marvellous ambassador for our country and a fine footballer. But he has promised not to bring me on as a substitute. So if the Albanians look like scoring I think I'll just wander on and try to put up a deckchair in the goalmouth.'

A win over Germany is rare enough. But David captained England to their biggest ever away win over their old footballing rivals – the 5-1 victory in Munich in the World Cup qualifier on September

Alan Shearer believes that you never truly realise how great Beckham is until you play alongside him.

1, 2001, which included a hat-trick from Michael Owen. David, who had played a part in the lead-up to two of the goals, was as astonished by the margin of victory as anybody. 'When the world sees this, they will probably be as amazed as we are,' he commented after the game. 'We all sat in the dressing room and said: "What's gone on there?" If you watch the faces when the third, fourth and fifth goals went in, all the players were thinking, *What the hell is going on?* But we have proved that we can come to places like this and perform at that level.'

> 'Becks has been brilliant as captain. He's a great influence in the way he deals with the pressure he's under. He turns a lot of negatives into positives, and you can really look up to him as a role model.'
> Rio Ferdinand, Leeds and England defender

David wears a new pair of Adidas boots for all key games, such as England internationals. In an average season of 50 games, he will wear approximately 30 pairs of boots. After Brooklyn was born, Adidas stitched the little boy's name into his father's boots. David has kept every pair. David said: 'I like the look of new boots and I feel good in new boots.' But if he has played well in a pair he will hang onto them for the next game. 'I used to give some of the old ones with "Becks" on the tongue away to charity or back to Adidas but since I had "Brooklyn" on the tongue I don't give them away any more.'

GREECE 2 – ENGLAND 1. ONE MINUTE TO PLAY...

After David Beckham led England to that stunning victory over the Germans, England required a victory over Greece to ensure a place in the 2002 World Cup Finals.

The match was played on October 6, 2001, at Beckham's 'home' ground, Old Trafford, Manchester, and the nation confidently expected England to win. But as the match drew to a conclusion, the home team were 2-1 down with the clock ticking away to the final whistle. Then England were awarded a free-kick. Teddy Sheringham, who had come on as a substitute and had immediately scored, was keen to take the free-kick. But Beckham, who had failed to convert several other free-kicks in the game, ushered him away, preferring to take the responsibility himself. By now the nation, almost to a man watching the game on TV, knew that Germany, not England, would go through if England could not pull the game back to 2-2. Beckham's free-kick was giving England one

> **'I don't think you realise quite how good David Beckham is until you play alongside him. He can do so many things with a football. He's got the world at his feet.'**
> Former England captain Alan Shearer

> **'We are aware, of course, that we might go down as legends but we have to keep our feet on the ground. But if we carry on like this we can go a long way.'**
> David Beckham, after England's 5-1 defeat of Germany

136

David Beckham knows how to charm the Germans as well as beating them. After leading the England team to their historic 5-1 World Cup qualifying win over Germany he dazzled them with an appearance on a top-rated chat show. Even after that famous victory David and his wife Victoria were greeted to a warm and noisy reception from the audience. German coach Rudi Voller praised England's skipper as: 'A great guy and a great footballer'. David told them modestly: 'I'm just a regular bloke.' And the Germans reacted very well to his comments about all of his success being down to his parents and a great deal of hard work. Victoria informed the rapt audience that she was not very good at housework although she did her best. Victoria said: 'David changes nappies and he is very handy with the vacuum cleaner. It is very hard to juggle family life with a career but you just have to get on with things and make the best of it.'

last chance and the nation held its breath as he placed the ball and looked up to see where to aim. The clock showed 93 minutes – three minutes of injury time had been played.

Teddy Sheringham was quick to praise his captain after the match. 'David struck gold with that shot,' he told the press. 'He played like a skipper today – in a poor team performance. My goal was important, but it wasn't the most important goal. The captain did that when we needed it. He ran himself into the ground.' England coach Sven Goran

Eriksson was equally unstinting in his praise: 'It seems incredible that David has struck that amazing free-kick which has taken us through to the World Cup. I knew it had finished 0-0 in Germany just before he was going to take it. David wanted to win the game so badly and showed he is a big captain for the side.'

Fellow England star Michael Owen said simply, 'The game belongs to David Beckham. If you are that good, you are always going to come out the hero and David has proved that once again.'

David's sister Joanne couldn't make it to Old Trafford for the crucial qualifier and watched the match at the family home in Chingford. 'I didn't even have any friends round because I just couldn't bear the tension,' she admitted afterwards. 'Mum phoned me crying as the team were doing their lap of honour.

'With players like David Beckham you feel there are certain moments of destiny. And Beckham takes the free-kick, arguably the most recognisable footballer in the world... Yes! Yes for England! And David Beckham has done it! Big time!'

Martin Tyler, Sky Sports commentator, as Beckham took his famous free-kick

It was a very emotional moment. I am so proud to be David's sister. I'm over the moon and so are my entire family.'

The excitement at Beckham's match-winning free-kick infected the whole country. And you didn't have to be a football fan to tell that something special had happened. Hollywood movie actress and Pirelli Calendar girl Monet

'It was always going to be on the script that he would take us to a World Cup, and maybe he can win it for us.'
Liverpool and England star Michael Owen on David Beckham's last-minute free-kick against Greece

Mazur, who came to London soon afterwards to promote the Pirelli 2002 calendar, revealed 'Everyone was talking about David Beckham. Who was David Beckham? I'm American and I wasn't sure who he was because I don't know anything about football. Then I realised he was the husband of that Spice Girl Victoria. He sure is a great looking guy,' she added, 'very sexy.'

Former Spice Girl Geri Halliwell reckoned David's last-minute goal against Greece helped her to stage one of the performances of her life. Geri was in the Omani desert waiting to perform in front of 7,000 British troops on a goodwill visit to cheer them up as they trained for possible war in Afghanistan. She was due to go on stage just after the end of the England-Greece game and feared she'd have to face a gloomy audience as all the squaddies knew England were losing 2-1. Then came David's goal. 'I have David to thank for making it a great show,' she said.

'David Beckham produced a great moment in football. I think we all jumped out of our chairs... He's such a wonderful talent and I haven't seen a better performance from a captain in a long time.'
Steve Bruce, former Manchester United captain

What about the man

David's goal from a free kick against Greece was voted by BBC TV viewers as the Golden TV Moment of 2001. David's last gasp effort polled 66% of the public's votes beating, among others, the shooting of Phil Mitchell in the soap EastEnders. John Motson, who was commentating on the match for the BBC, said: 'As things stood in injury time and Greece were leading 2-1, England were in a predicament where they were heading for the play-offs. When Beckham scored, Trevor Brooking and I lost it completely. We both jumped up from our seats and we ran down the gantry towards the nearest cameraman and started to hug him. It was probably the most thrilling and dramatic moment I've experienced in 30 years of television commentary because all of a sudden England were sexy again.' Accepting the award, David said: 'It's the best sporting moment of my career.'

himself? Naturally, he was ecstatic at the victory – but more for what the result meant for the team than for any solo glory. 'The whole nation was lifted by qualifying for the World Cup,' he beamed. 'Achieving it so late against Greece made it even better. It was fate being given those extra minutes to salvage our World Cup dreams.' But, crucially, he maintained that any future England glory had to be built on a concerted team effort rather than individual moments of brilliance. 'We have to play better,' he insisted. 'To beat the Germans 5-1 in their own backyard is a result that has gone down in history; but we have to play every game like

Geri Halliwell, who was grateful to David for his
eleventh-hour magic against Greece as it helped warm
up the audience before a gig!

that. There are certain nations, like Argentina and France, you look up to and we have to get up to their level. Argentina have a young team with a lot of good players and France are always going to be a threat.'

An effigy of David Beckham was hung up outside a south London pub after England's World Cup defeat in 1998. Clearly some of the regulars at The Pleasant Pheasant in South Norwood blamed David's sending off for England's exit from the finals. But the mood of the pub had changed full circle when his free-kick against Greece went in. Bar manager Anne Marie Callear revealed: 'The place went absolutely mad when the equaliser went in. It was full of England supporters and most of them had given up hope. No-one could believe it. Then they started singing out Beckham's name. It was brilliant.'

Piers Morgan, editor of the *Mirror*, recalls: 'When he was sent off, we all just thought, *'You stupid boy.'* That was our headline: Ten Heroic Lions, One Stupid Boy. But – and it's a big but – this guy has come back from the abyss of his career. He's the great British lionheart. It's no wonder that papers like the *Mirror* call for him to be Sir Goldenballs, as we now like to dub him. He epitomises all that's great about being British.'

⚽ **'He epitomises all that's great about being British.'**

David Beckham has certainly won some impressive admirers since entering the top flight of football. Take this comment from Franz Beckenbauer, the man who led West Germany to the take the World Cup in 1974, and now the president of Bayern Munich: 'Coming from a German, this is going to sound a little controversial. But my vote for the world's best footballer, if I had one, would go to Beckham. David Beckham is simply the most exciting, talented footballer in the world. He can continue to get better. I really like him. I like the way he passes the ball and the way he shoots. It's fantastic. As long as they have Beckham in the team, England will always have a chance of making progress.'

Praise doesn't come much higher than that. And it looks as though Goldenballs will be on the England scene for some time to come. Indeed, former England No. 2 John Gorman argues that David is already on course to rewrite the record books, overtake Peter Shilton's 125 appearances and become England's most capped player. Glenn Hoddle called up Beckham after he replaced Terry Venables as national team coach in 1996 and gave the youngster his first cap in a World Cup qualifier against Moldova. 'We knew straight away he would be a permanent fixture in our team,' Gorman said. 'Moldova wasn't exactly Portugal or Germany but it was a tricky game away from home and the pitch was awful. But you could see the excitement in his eyes. We hadn't had a chance to play him in a friendly. But we knew he wouldn't let us down and he didn't. David can be anything he wants to be. If he continues to show the same desire for England as he did under us, he can carry on playing for years and years.'

CHAPTER 5

BECKHAM
THE ICON

TO MANY people, David Beckham is much, much more than just a successful footballer. Dr Mark Griffiths, Psychologist at Nottingham Trent University, believes there are a number of reasons why we find him so fascinating. 'He's been around since his childhood. He has been on television since he was a young boy and has grown up in the public eye,' he argues. 'He has a "unisex" appeal. He is a very talented footballer, which appeals to men, and also possesses a boyish charm, which appeals to women. He's good looking and rich. Of course, the money aspect is phenomenal and we are always interested in rich people. This combined with his good looks and talent are irresistible. After all, if he looked like Peter Beardsley I don't think he'd be so popular!

⚽ **'David Beckham's image reaches right across the globe.'**

'David Beckham's image reaches right across the globe,' Dr Griffiths continues. 'Manchester United are known throughout the world, and he is probably their greatest player, so naturally people are drawn to him. David is one half of an extremely high-profile celebrity partnership. The fact that he is married to an internationally renowned pop star adds to this attraction; everyone likes to support something that is successful. This international recognition is one of the differences between the Beckhams and, say, the Redknapps. Louise Redknapp is very popular here but is not well known outside the country, and while Jamie Redknapp is a talented footballer he is simply not in the same league as Beckham. Of course, there is also an element of choice: the Beckhams court publicity while the Redknapps choose to remain more anonymous.

'People like celebrity couples because of the sexual and romantic elements involved. There is also a ⚽ **'They are pseudo-royals.'** strong jealousy and we are often pleased to see the rich and famous knocked down a peg or two either by failing in a relationship or losing their status. There may be an element of waiting to see what will go wrong with Posh and Becks, although I actually think they are very good together. They are pseudo-royals; the thrones and crowns at their wedding coupled with "Beckingham Palace" implies that, to some people, they are on a par with the royal family in the things they do.

'There are several important defining moments in David Beckham's life and he seems to be rated by the public over single incidents. He is a hero when he scores a stunning goal (such as in the game against Greece) and completely vilified when he makes a mistake, the obvious example being when England were knocked out of the World Cup by Argentina.

Whenever he makes a single change of hairstyle, or shaves his eyebrow, the nation sits up and takes notice. He was voted Sports Personality of the Year because of the excellent performance he gave against Greece. He has grown enormously in humility and maturity over recent years. In the last World Cup Beckham was very young and impetuous, but since then respect for him has grown and grown. If he ran for prime minister we would vote for him, such is his popularity.'

⚽ **'He has matured greatly since becoming England captain, which I think is reflected in his looks.'**

Dr Griffiths regards David's faux pas against Argentina as a major influence on his subsequent career: 'The World Cup experience was very humbling for him,' he argues. 'He took it on board and learned from it; it's very rare now that we see him put a foot wrong. He has matured greatly since becoming England captain, which I think is reflected in his looks; the fact he has got rid of his boyish long hair, for example.'

'The fact that he has matured is reflected not only in the media but also in impressionist portrayals of him,' Dr Griffiths observes. 'In the Alistair McGowan sketches, he appears to be the clever one while Posh is depicted as more and more stupid.' As it happened, Beckham had all his hair cut off, just before comedian Alistair McGowan's first TV series – which was a little inconvenient for the impressionist, who plays one half of the well-known 'Posh and Becks' skit. 'I'm not equating it to the Kennedy shooting,' McGowan says, 'but I know exactly where I was when I heard that

David Beckham had had all his hair cut off. I was at the gym in Clapham and thought: That's 20 minutes of material down the toilet!'

Dr Griffiths continues: 'It would seem that anyone who mocks him is simply jealous, as Beckham does very little that is controversial. He is very serious about his family and has taken on the role of Alan Shearer – not only in the England captaincy but in his family values. I think he will remain successful, even after his career as a footballer is over. A lot of youngsters only know Gary Lineker from *Match of the Day* and the Walkers crisps adverts. Gary Lineker's career has gone from strength to strength and I think that Beckham will follow a similar pattern. Financially he never needs to work again but I'm sure he will remain in the public eye for many years to come.'

> **'I really enjoy doing Posh and Becks. I've heard them say on chat shows how much they like my spoof. It shows they are a couple who have learned to laugh at themselves.'**
>
> Impressionist Alistair McGowan

Make no mistake, there are people who take the whole idea of David Beckham *very* seriously indeed. Fancy a BA in Beckham? David's tears, tantrums and hairstyles have been put under the floodlight in a football culture module offered as part of a university degree course. Students taking Culture, Media and Sports Studies at Staffordshire University scrambled to sign up for the 12-week course to study their idol. His relationship with his wife inevitably forms part of the module, along with his latest haircuts and

Robbie Williams admires
the way David handles
the down sides of his
extraordinary fame.

the impact of his sending-off against Argentina in the World Cup. Course lecturer Professor Ellis Cashmore – an Aston Villa supporter sees him as 'the icon of icons. We may even begin to gauge our times by his haircuts or his sendings-off. Nobody embodies the spirit of our times as well as David Beckham.' Professor Cashmore believes that the footballer has a cultural significance that will last for years to come. 'The Beckham phenomenon is inescapable,' he maintains. 'It's not quite like JFK, but we are getting to the stage where people will say, "Where were you when David Beckham was sent off?"' Ellis cashmore's own book, *Beckham*, will be published by Polity in the latter half of 2002.

As we have seen, David Beckham has reached the pinnacle of the footballing world through a mixture of exceptional natural talent and hard work. His daunting perfectionism is an object lesson for any would-be football star. A fascinating insight into that almost obsessive attention to detail was borne out by an ITV documentary on him, in which it emerged that David Beckham is a remarkably neat person. Everything in his homes has to be perfectly clean and tidy. He cannot relax if there is a speck of dust anywhere and even when he is in hotel rooms he makes sure everything is just so. Ian Denyer, who spent six months following David for the documentary, revealed: 'His flat is white on white and he wears white at home. He knows it's mad but he can't help it.' David was also shown to only allow even numbers of cola cans in the fridge, to arrange objects at right angles to each other and to file his shirts in a colour-coded straight line.

Denyer added: 'In a hotel room we see David rearrange

things to suit his obsession. It's a very funny sequence. He immediately pounces on cable TV cards and puts them in a drawer. He makes perfect arrangements of things. The DVD player has to be parallel to the edge of the table. He was fretting that the maid had moved a bottle of water so he had to move it back again.' The striving for perfection that helps to make David Beckham one of the greatest footballers in the world also seem to make him do odd things at times. But Denyer was also clear on one thing. He most certainly loves his wife. Denyer said: 'The hour after Victoria leaves David

Pop Stars personality Darius Danesh.

R & B superstar Usher – one of David's favourite musicians.

is very deflated. He is not a gregarious, out-on-the-town type, having blondes sit in his lap. He is a shy, retiring man with few close friends. I have never met a man more in love with his wife that David Beckham, and David is also the most placid man I have ever met.'

Some of David's greatest admirers are pretty well known themselves. Pop star Robbie Williams is experienced at handling fame but he reckons if he attracted the attention from the media and the fans that David Beckham gets it could send him crazy. 'I am one of David Beckham's biggest fans,' the ex-Take That star once revealed. 'He deals with stuff much better than I would. I think the whole thing with him is awful. He is very good-looking and very rich. He is a fantastic footballer who has a good-looking wife and child. He has what everyone wants, so therefore everyone hates him. I would be getting into the crowd and fighting with people if I got the abuse he does. I find it very unfortunate for him. But he handles himself very well and he deals with stuff like a grown-up. He can handle the flak better than me. He rises above it.'

His sentiments are shared by inspirational Liverpool and England star Steven Gerrard: 'Everyone enjoys playing with Beckham, and I think he and I complement each other well. You always look to give the ball to the danger man, that's why we always look for Becks when we've got the ball. He's a great role model, the way he deals with his fame.'

> 'The way Beckham has turned his career around has been absolutely incredible. He's an inspiration. Off the field he's a style icon and his clothes are testament to a man who has a lot of balls... He's a real trendsetter, whether it be the haircut, the ear-piercing, the clothes... Much respect to the man.'
>
> Darius Danesh, star of TV's hit talent show Pop Idol

Although popular *Cold Feet* star James Nesbitt is not gay, he's not afraid to admit that he is hopelessly devoted to David Beckham. 'I'm in love with David Beckham,' the football-loving actor admits. 'There is a deep homophobia where I come from, but I never had a problem with homosexuality. I just thought that there wasn't a homosexual gene in my body. But… I do think if there was a crisis in the world that could only be solved by me kissing David, I would probably do it. I love him that much.'

Naturally, David Beckham has heroes of his own and among the singers he most

'David Beckham is my ultimate hero. I have met some of the biggest names in music but David is the main man.'

admires is award-winning American R&B star Usher, and it turns out that the feeling is mutual. The two men met after England's vital final World Cup qualification game against Greece at Old Trafford. David was already euphoric after scoring the crucial late goal that snatched a draw and took England to the finals, and he was delighted when Usher was there after the game to share the moment. Wearing a Beckham England shirt the singer enthused: 'David Beckham is my ultimate hero. I have met some of the biggest names in music but David is the main man. He played brilliantly and to meet him afterwards was a real honour. We chatted about football and music. This is the first game I have been to and I am totally blown away. The atmosphere was amazing. I've never experienced anything like it.'

Of course, when you become as famous as David Beckham there's a price to pay. Privacy is a rare and valuable commodity when virtually every day there's something about you in the press or someone who wants their picture taken with you. One of David's favourite restaurants is the Ivy in London, where autograph hunters are definitely not on the menu. 'We don't go there to be flash,' says David. 'When we visit some places we can't eat because people are continually coming up and asking for autographs. We rarely turn down autograph requests, but it is nice to finish a meal sometimes before it gets cold. In the Ivy they don't let anyone ask for autographs. I know this because Michael Jordan was in there one night and I was not able to get his signature.'

JAPAN AND THE WORLD CUP

The excitement ahead of the World Cup is building up in the Far East and most of the Oriental enthusiasm is directed towards the England captain. Beckham fan Junichiro Takebe says: 'This country will go crazy when David Beckham arrives. He is like a god in Japan. People admire his skills and they love the way he conducts himself. He is his own man in every situation. Japanese people like his strength of character and his strong identification with family values. They see his fantastic free-kicks and they cheer but they also cheer when he has his baby son Brooklyn on his shoulder and his wife by his side. In his book David Beckham wrote of importance of family. Both his mother and father and that of his wife Victoria are happy together in big family unit. Japanese supporters believe that helps to make him a good captain for England. He is in the newspaper headlines all the time, but not for bad things like drinking and fighting like some other footballers.'

⚽ **When it comes to Japanese girls, they vote David Beckham every time.**

In Japan, David Beckham and Michael Owen are the best known of all the England players. Young Japanese boys admire Michael Owen for his remarkable scoring feats and David Beckham for his fine leadership qualities. But when it comes to Japanese girls, they vote David Beckham every time. 'Michael Owen is big because of the goal he scored against Argentina in the last World Cup,'

> **'England are based in Japan in the first round and the reaction here will be absolutely huge. The teenage girls will be camped outside the airport when he flies in.'**
> Kosuke Inagaki from Japanese newspaper *Asahi Shunbun*

explains Kosuke Inagaki from Tokyo's national daily paper *Asahi Shunbun*, 'but Beckham is much more than just a footballer.'

Female Japanese fan Maki Takahara reveals: 'I have David Beckham posters covering every inch of my bedroom walls and so do some of my friends. He is supercool, so skilful and so handsome. He is the ideal man for us because he is also so caring and kind. He is strong and brave on the pitch but gentle and protective to his family off it... When he had the mohican haircut I bought 10 copies of a magazine with the photograph and I have them covering the inside of my bedroom door. Every morning I kiss them. I have never been a fan of anyone before, but now I devote my whole life to David Beckham. I am not a crazy lovesick person and one day I want to be a lawyer, but now David Beckham is everything. Me and my friends will be at the airport waiting just to get a brief glimpse of him.'

A MAN WITH STYLE

David Beckham has set new precedents in many different areas, including his insistence on putting his family above all else – even football – and his adventurous approach to fashion. Put simply, he dares to be different. He knows perfectly well that the popular image of professional footballers is not a terribly attractive one. But David is living proof that not all successful soccer stars are loud, lager-fuelled lunatics.

> ⚽ **His idea of a great night is snuggling up at home with Victoria, a video and a Chinese take-away.**

He prefers a glass of wine to a can of lager any day, and his idea of a great night is snuggling up at home with Victoria, a video and a Chinese take-away.

When he was seven years old David was asked to be a pageboy at a wedding and his mum warned him that this would mean wearing a frilly shirt and the sort of outfit that some of his pals might take the mickey out of. David didn't care a jot. He is so confident in himself that people teasing him does not upset him at all.

Although he is happily heterosexual himself, David was not at all unhappy that he has a large following from gays. Victoria said that her husband has been very flattered by the appreciation he's won from the gay community. Adam Mattera, editor of the leading gay lifestyle magazine *Attitude* observes: 'David is incredibly popular among gay men for many reasons. He isn't just a good-looking bloke. He is not gay looking, he's straight, but there is simply not than macho man thing about him. He reminds you of the famous Athena poster print with the man cradling the baby showing how it is cool to be a father and to be caring. The other thing is that he is totally in on the fashion scene. He's got great taste in clothes and isn't afraid to be darting about clothes either. Also, it's great that he hasn't got any hang-ups about being friends with gay people – he's far too cool to be like that. You see him mixing with people like Elton John and George Michael with the same ease as a fellow footballer.'

Contrary to most of the reports, it was David's idea, not Victoria's, for him to wear the Gaultier sarong that caused so much controversy. David had bought it while out shopping in Paris with Spice Girl Mel B's ex-husband Jimmy Gulzar. After David was famously photographed wearing it, he phoned his father. Ted Beckham's response was: 'What on earth is that?' David replied: 'It's one of those wrap-around things.'

> 'He's a man with a great eye for goal, a perfect pass, an exciting eye for fashion and style. The eyes of the world are on this man and no more so than this year, 2002, World Cup year. I hope his sunglasses can take a little bit of the glare off this man this year.'
>
> Gabby Logan at David's launch of a new range of Police sunglasses in London, February 2002

'You Jessie, you'll look like a blimmin' tart!' Ted retorted. But when he saw the pictures in the papers he changed his mind: 'I thought he looked smart,' his father admitted. 'I rather liked it.'

David is not only an icon of the footballing world, but of the fashion world too. Here he is shown modelling Police sunglasses - for which he was paid a cool £1 million.

Of course, it does tend to help you to carry off bold fashion statements if you're drop-dead gorgeous. Silvia Nanni says that when they were getting ready to do the first photo-shoot with David for Police sunglasses, all sorts of clothing, shirts and jackets had been prepared for him to wear in front of the cameras. 'But,' says Silvia, 'David came out wearing just jeans and came straight to me and said: "OK, what would you like me to wear?" And I went very girlish and said: "Nothing, David, you look fantastic the way you are."'

> 'I want to help create the kind of clothes which I would have wanted to wear when I was younger.'
>
> David Beckham

And it seems that kids in the high street will soon be able to benefit from David's keen fashion sense: he is joining forces with Marks & Spencer to launch a new range of casual clothing for boys. The fashion range, featuring co-ordinating tops, bottoms and accessories, will be launched exclusively in Marks & Spencer stores in the autumn. David will work with an M & S design team to create a collection of separates for boys aged between 6 and 14 and will lend his name and image to the range. 'For some time now I've been enjoying the creative side of my commercial work,' he revealed to the press, 'and when Marks & Spencer offered me the opportunity to actively assist in the design of clothing for youngsters, I was delighted.' 'David Beckham is the perfect icon for this boyswear range,' maintains Michele Jobling, Managing Director of the Marks & Spencer Zip

Project. 'Not only is he the number one sporting hero for all boys from the age they begin to kick a football, but he is also a great style icon and role model.'

David Beckham only has to get a new jacket to hit the headlines. But when he wore a motorcycle outfit with a cigarette logo, he had the anti-smoking lobby up in arms. David was photographed wearing the leather jacket, with 'Lucky Strike' emblazoned across the back as he watched wife Victoria filming a pop video. Clive Bates, director of Action on Smoking and Health, was not impressed: 'I am absolutely disgusted, especially as I am a Man United fan and a big admirer of Beckham. One of the most popular footballers in the world has put himself behind something which is the basic opposite of smoking achievement. It is especially shocking because he is a new father. Children are twice as likely to smoke if their parents do and 13,000 youngsters a year are admitted to hospital with respiratory problems because their parents smoke. This is a terrible example to set.' But no one is more protective of his family than David Beckham and a spokesman for the star explained: 'It is just an old classic Fifties insignia. David is not advocating smoking. He doesn't smoke.'

> **'A macho role model who is not afraid of fashion or of being attractive and showing off his body.'**
>
> Tom Ford, designer for Yves St Laurent and Gucci, on David Beckham

Equally as famous as his sarong or his trend-setting hairstyles are David's tattoos. Louis Molloy decorated the most famous torso in British football at his tattooist's studio in Middleton, Manchester. 'I'd been working on some of David's team-mates and one of them gave me an indication David would be getting in touch with me,' he explained. 'Sure enough, he came in and I did some sketches for him while he was here. Later he came in and approved one. It was the one on his back which has come to be known as the guardian angel tattoo. I also did the tattoo on his arm of Victoria's name in Hindi. There was a lot of fuss that it wasn't spelled correctly but we couldn't get a direct translation so it's a phonetic translation. David was very happy with it.

'He comes in on a regular basis when I've always got other clients here,' Louis continues. 'He's always got time for them and for the kids waiting outside for his autograph. He's a nice bloke. It's a real buzz for me to see him running out on to the pitch as captain of England knowing that he's got my tattoos under his shirt. It's also amazing for me when he does photo-shoots for magazines and the photos of him with my tattoos are going out all over the world.' Beckham also had his son's name Brooklyn tattooed on his lower back – so that the guardian angel is looking over him.

What about that barnet? David Beckham was well aware he was following another sporting hero when he was signed up by Brylcreem in 1997. Denis Compton, who played cricket for Middlesex and football for Arsenal, was the original 'Brylcreem Boy' and David said: 'Denis Compton is a massive sporting hero and my granddad has told me all about him.' Of course, in those days the Beckham locks

David's healthy energetic lifestyle means that he never needs to diet. He can eat what he likes without worrying about putting weight on. One of his favourite meals is bacon and egg sandwiches with lashings of tomato sauce all over them. He sometimes wakes up in the early hours of the morning and has that or just tea and toast, and he loves McDonald's.

were long and blonde, and being copied on every high street in the land. Then – wouldn't you know it – he shaved his head, and promptly sparked off another haircut craze. And when David had two lines cut in his hair, and later in his left eyebrow, thousands of kids copied that, too. But what did the lines signify? David was not saying, but fans insist one is for Brooklyn and one is for Victoria.

David appeared in *The Face* in June 2001 in a photograph that unveiled another new look – a mohican haircut – and what looked like blood dripping down his forehead. Naturally, the psychologists had a field day. Professor Alex Gardner asked: 'Does Beckham's menacing, hard-edged pose show an identification with dark obsession?' (To get the right effect for the dramatic photos, David poured a bottle of soy sauce over his head.) The mohican haircut had been inspired by the one Robert De Niro sported as Travis Bickle in the hit film *Taxi Driver*. It shocked a lot of people at the time, and even Sir Alex

Ferguson was moved to suggest it was becoming a distraction. David thought it looked 'wicked' but he agreed that the publicity and attention it was attracting was out of all proportion, and he agreed that he did not need any more abuse.

Of course, his radical new haircut had a few very public outings on the football pitch first, and elsewhere, for that matter. Keen football fan the Duke of Devonshire was surprised when David Beckham, complete with new mohican, and his wife Victoria visited the Royal Opera House in July 2001 to watch the Kirov Ballet. Posh and Becks took all four seats in a box to preserve their privacy on their second wedding anniversary. The Duke said: 'I had no idea they were ballet fans. I didn't actually see them myself but I wish I had as I rather fancy his new hairstyle. Unfortunately,' the Duke sighed, 'I haven't got any hair at all these days.'

NEW MAN

It's not going too far to say that David Beckham is personally responsible for making it fashionable to be a caring father and faithful husband. The new man with old values has had a huge effect on men's behaviour, according to a survey for FHM Bionic. David's frank and open enthusiasm for marriage, his love for his wife and his devotion to their son had an enormous impact on young men of today, according to the magazine's survey of 3,000 men across the United Kingdom. The survey concluded that

169

men were being sparked into meaningful relationships and away from one-night stands. The figures showed that a staggering 88 per cent of those questioned want love and affection and there was a massive move towards romance and away from the lager-driven laddish society.

The message has clearly got through to our transatlantic cousins too. 'There is nothing more beautiful in the English game than the sight of one of Mr. Beckham's free-kicks arching over the defenders' wall and curling into the corner of the net, or one of his signature cross shots cannonading off his foot and speeding like a guided missile toward one of his leaping team-mates to be headed across the line for a goal,' observes Warren Hoge of the *New York Times*. 'Mr Beckham has the sculptured good looks of a silent movie star. He is shamelessly physical with his son, hugging and kissing Brooklyn at every photo opportunity and further endearing himself to women, who never imagined that they would find a feeling man in the midst of a lager-swilling soccer culture.'

'Beckham makes most Premiership footballers look like overgrown schoolboys,' insisted Tony Parsons in the *Mirror* on December 17, 2001. 'It is impossible to imagine

> **'The family man is cool again. Beckham more than anyone personifies the new Dad – not the old Dad who bought his clothes from a camping shop and spent his spare time on an allotment.'**
>
> Phil Hilton, *FHM Bionic* editor

David's love of fast cars is almost an obsession!

Father and son celebrate
Manchester United clinching
another League title.

Beckham beating up his girlfriend (like Stan Collymore), getting legless in front of people mourning the carnage of September 11 (like Frank Lampard) or going mental in McDonald's because he couldn't get a quarter pounder at six in the morning (like Lee Bowyer).'

⚽ **David likes his toys as much as any man and there's no doubt that cars are one of the great loves of his life.**

That said, David likes his toys as much as any man and there's no doubt that cars are one of the great loves of his life. He enjoys selecting the right colour and choosing which of the many extras to have. 'I probably sound like a flash git and that is something that I have probably got wrong with me,' he confesses. 'But as long as I am not letting the players down I can live my life the way I want.' David's first car was a bright red Ford Escort, which he acquired when he was 17 and just starting to make his mark at Manchester United. He loved it. Since then he has owned some of the finest cars in the world but he says the thrill of driving off on his own in his very first car still takes a lot of beating. David bought a blue £80,000 Porsche after he signed his first boot deal. He also has a hankering for a fast motorcycle. Once he spotted a 170 mph Ducati 996 and soon found himself drooling over its astonishing performance. The bike accelerates from 0 to 60 mph in just 2.8 seconds, and up to 135 mph in just 12 seconds. But David knows that such a purchase would probably alarm both Sir Alex Ferguson and his wife Victoria. So he has put that particular purchase on hold. For the time being.

Lest we forget, although he's become a new role model for men, Beckham has always proved a sizeable hit with the ladies too. A survey for website asSeenonScreen for Valentine's Day 2001 named Becks as the man whom most women would like to date. 'It was no surprise that David Beckham came out on top in our Valentine's Day survey as he's hugely popular,' admitted a spokesperson for the website. 'He is one of the stars who heavily influence what people buy from us, such as his sunglasses, parka and jewellery. And I think he'd win again if we carried out another survey – he's even more popular now than he was back then.'

In fact, David Beckham comes top of most popularity polls. But on one occasion, he was beaten by actor Russell Crowe in a survey on manliness. Psychologist June McNicholas interviewed 200 women to rate the two men out of ten for manliness. Russell scored seven while David registered just five. 'I showed participants a picture of David Beckham in a headscarf and Russell Crowe sporting designer stubble,' the psychologist explained. 'I was surprised to find women of all ages snubbing Becks. Many thought he looked like a camp pirate.' The survey concluded that women were turning their backs on 'new age' man of the 1990s who spent ages preening himself in front of the mirror. Dr McNicholas, who did her survey in the Midlands, said: 'Women today don't want tears and tantrums over the slightest thing. They want real men who look the part.'

Well, perhaps. But when the authors of this book

conducted a similar survey they found David Beckham got twice as many women's votes as Russell Crowe…

CHAPTER 6

THE FAME GAME

DAVID BECKHAM refuses to allow his phenomenal fame to go to his head. Even back in 1996 when he was just establishing himself in the team the 21-year-old stated firmly: 'People keep asking if all this adulation is frightening and when am I going to get carried away. It won't happen. It can't with so many people keeping my feet on the ground. I love the success, to be honest. I love signing autographs and I accept the demands of being in the public eye. I used to rush round getting autographs when I was a kid, so I understand how they feel. Now it is just part of the job and one I like doing. Everything for me at the moment is a dream come true.'

Well, he might be keeping a cool head about things, but the rest of the world seems to have gone Beckham-crazy. If you don't believe it, take a look at a few items from the papers that show what people are prepared to get up to in the name of Beckham…

NOTTINGHAM VICAR, Reverend Andy Bruce, from Mansfield Road Baptist Church, surprised many of

'God forgives even David Beckham'

his more staid parishioners when he put a sign outside his church saying 'God forgives even David Beckham' after his sending off in the Argentina game in France 1998. But the vicar was undaunted by whispers of criticism and after the Greece game this year he followed up his public footballing poster sermon with a sign that read: 'Becks: see what a little forgiveness can do'. 'It is so easy for footballers to go from hero to villain and back to hero again in a very short space of time,' Bruce explained. 'I think David Beckham has proved that it's important to give people second chances. All of the blame was heaped on him after the Argentina match which was unfair, and I think he's made a remarkable comeback. He was extremely young at the time and he's grown up a lot since then. Since becoming England captain he's been even more impressive and he's proved the importance of forgiveness.'

DAVID BECKHAM is the most popular computer password in Great Britain, ahead of Homer Simpson, Keanu Reeves and Madonna, reported a nationwide survey of office workers. But users are warned that using the name of Britain's best soccer player to access their computer could not be the greatest security device. Computer expert Davies Munro said: 'If you see a work station covered with photos of David Beckham it might not take the greatest technological wizard on earth to deduce what the password might be.'

DAVID BECKHAM, Alan Smith, David James and Luis Figo are in hot soup in Bangkok's throbbing Chinatown. Meat balls named after the soccer stars are boiled and then served with noodles to queues of customers. Each dish has been named, after the personal preferences of the vendor's family members, to reflect the players' traits. David Beckham is a youthful 'fresh meat' dish, Alan Smith is a hard-kicking meat ball, David James a clumsy meat stew and Luis Figo the speciality of the house, that reflects his status as the world's most expensively acquired player. But customer Bernard Cartwright returned to Britain to say: 'The David Beckham meat balls were easily the best. Luis Figo's seemed a little overdone and past their best. Rather like the player.'

CURRY HOUSE staff went to extraordinary lengths to prove there's naan like David Beckham when they wanted their hero named as England captain. The ten workers from the Bengal Dynasty in Clwyd honoured the sizzling footballer by naming a curry after him: the Beckhamdaloo. 'We wanted to show how much we admire him,' said waiter Angur Miah, 27. 'It's got devil chillies in it and is as hot as David is right now.' And not only did David prove to be a tasty dish, he inspired his own band of spice boys at the restaurant. All ten staff had their heads shaved in a number one haircut as a tribute to their own favourite number seven. Regular customers saw the funny side as the staff all lined up sporting the same infamous hairstyle. Angur, the first to have his head shaved, was followed into the barbers by chef Fokrul Islam and fellow waiters Yousuf Uddin, Monchab Ali, Surat Miah, Islam Uddin, Mohammed Enam, Kobir Ahmed, Nojmul Hoque and Fotik Miah.

IN APRIL 2000, ska duo Ian St Peters and Campbell Downie released a record called 'She Only Fancies Him Cos He Looks Like David Beckham'.

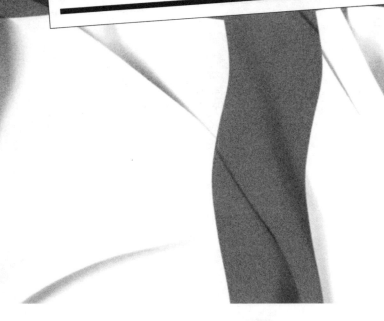

THE THOUGHT THAT ONE DAY it might really be possible to clone a human being has caused much controversy. The successful cloning of sheep and monkeys has sparked much heated debate and some believe that it is only a matter of time before humans, especially footballers, are next. But Mr Ian Gibson, Labour member of Parliament's select committee on science and technology, told the BBC: 'I get letters from people thinking we are going to clone David Beckham. We are not going to do that.'

'I HAVE GOT GREAT ADMIRATION for him as a footballer, and it came as no surprise that he won the Sports Personality of the Year award. He has matured considerably since becoming England captain. He's got a positive mental attitude and his ability is second to none. I've sold quite a lot of the gnomes, especially as he's been in the limelight a lot lately.' Jeff Callaghan, creator of the Posh and Becks garden gnomes, a snip at £27.50 each.

ANDY HARMER, a former car washer from Eastbourne, Sussex, has had his life transformed by David Beckham's rise to super-stardom. Andy is a dead ringer for David, and his uncanny likeness has given him a new career as a full time lookalike working for the Splitting Image agency, where he's been earning up to £500 a time. Andy, 22, who reckons he shows no mean skill with a football himself, rates his best booking as the day he was used as a double for Beckham's Pepsi advert.

The impact of his extraordinary likeness to England's captain was really brought home to Andy the day he was at 'home', the trendy nightclub in London's Leicester Square. Andy's job on that occasion was to introduce the guests. He was so convincing that he was mistaken by many for the real thing. 'I was standing near a window,' he recalls, 'and when I looked around there were thousands of people staring up at me. The police were called and told me to move – I was creating pandemonium.'

Another lad who has benefited from having strikingly similar looks to Beckham is Mark Hyden from Staffordshire. The part-time model and music technology student was Beckham's body double in an advert for Adidas where Beckham is seen kicking a bag of chips into a bin. While filming the advert, a crowd of girls gathered in the street to watch Mark and started screaming his name. 'They said I was nicer than the real thing and had better legs,' says Mark. 'It was a bit embarrassing, really.'

A PAIR OF ADIDAS Predator football boots given by David Beckham to a fan who was accidentally hit in the face with a stray shot during the pre-match warm-up at Leicester City fetched £2,350 at Christie's in September 2001.

A MAN dressed in a blue ferret costume bought a pair of David Beckham's old football boots for £13,800 at an auction of Manchester United memorabilia at Christie's in London. The Adidas boots, worn by David during the 1997/98 season, had been expected to go for under £1,000. But the bidding went up and up until the blue ferret man bought them for a Swedish Internet company.

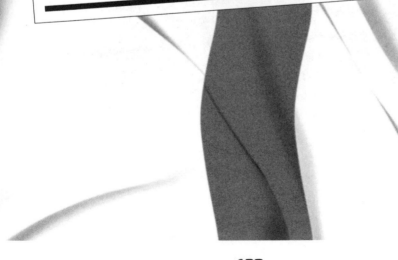

THE MONKS of Yak Chon Sa temple in Saegwipo, Jeju Island, are looking forward to seeing David in the World Cup in Korea. Sung Gong, chief monk of the temple, the biggest in Korea, said: 'We all saw Beckham's goal against Greece on television. Without him England might not be coming. We all know Beckham – he has the same haircut as me and the other monks. We also have a team called Sam Bo, which means 'Buddha'. I play on the right in midfield, like Beckham.'

HEAD ROY LUDLOW was not happy when members of the under-16 team at Beechen Hill School in Bath, Somerset copied the Beckham hairstyle. He said it made them look aggressive and yobbish and he decided they were unfit to represent the school. He sent them home for two days so they missed out on playing in the first round of the Somerset Cup. Local rivals from the Ralph Allen School went through to the second round on a default and Beechen Hill were unable to defend the cup they won in 1999.

One player, 15-year-old Ben Crane said: 'All we were trying to do was show unity. We did not want to offend the headmaster and only did it for our team. Now we will not have any more games to play this year.' Another player grumbled: 'If a haircut is good enough for an England star like Becks, surely it should be good enough for us?' But headmaster Ludlow was unrepentant. He said: 'They are good lads but their virtually shaved heads made them look aggressive and yobbish. They made a serious error of judgement.'

JOHN BRETT of Pigmania, Hereford: 'When the Spice Girls were promoting their movie, we made little model pigs of The Spice Girls. Then one day Jackie Adams, Victoria Beckham's mother, phoned me up and asked if I could make one of David Beckham. So I made one about six inches high of David in a Manchester United shirt. It took me about a week to design and I created it from a photograph of David. After she'd received it, Jackie Adams phoned me to say that David thought it was fantastic. He thought it was really wicked. Apparently he was so chuffed with his pig.'

AFTER MANCHESTER UNITED'S incredible Treble-winning triumph in 1999, Hasbro created a David Beckham doll. It was one of three dolls based on members of the Man U team, all created to mark the club's unprecedented success in winning the League Championship, the FA Cup and the Champions' League all in the same season. 'The doll was a great success,' says a Hasbro official.

DAVID CAME EIGHTH in a poll of readers of *Manchester United Magazine* to discover who were the club's 100 greatest players ever. The magazine polled its readers to pick The Official Manchester United 100 Greatest Players who deserved a place in Old Trafford's hall of fame and David was voted into eighth place behind Roy Keane (7), Bryan Robson (6), Peter Schmeichel (5), Bobby Charlton (4), Ryan Giggs (3), George Best (2), and Eric Cantona (1).

And in a very different kind of poll, the Sun named David as Sexiest Man In The World. Ryan Giggs came 34th.

DAVID BECKHAM pays a fortune in tax but he should pay even more insisted Labour MP Alan Simpson who attacked the 'obscene wealth' of the England captain and other high earners. Mr Simpson stirred up a wave of apathy when he stormed: 'When you start to talk to people about the superstar lifestyles, whether it is in the music industry of the salaries being paid weekly to the nation's footballers – the Beckhams of the world – the amount of money going to the super-rich is quite rightly viewed as obscene in itself. But it is grossly unfair when people who are on say, £40,000 a year, are in the same tax bracket with other people who are earning that amount per week.'

A NUMBER of stars queued up to sing David's praises on a fascinating BBC TV show called *There's Only One David Beckham*. Here's what they had to say:

ACTOR RICHARD E. GRANT: 'He's one of the few men other men talk of as dead-on handsome.'

ULRIKA JONSSON: 'I don't get the impression there's a vanity about him. I think he knows he's good looking – and he should. If he doesn't, I'll tell him.'

ANGUS DEAYTON, a big Manchester United fan, remembered that he first met David at Manchester airport when the team were flying out for a European tie – and David had managed to forget his passport. 'Now,' said Angus, 'he'd be able to walk into any country in the world and they wouldn't need to ask him for his passport. They'd probably just ask for his autograph.'

FASHION stylist Kenny Ho: 'He's the most stylish man in Britain.'

Boxing champ Prince Naseem Hamed: 'Basically he's got a gift from God – and he's using that gift.'

EX-ENGLAND footballer Paul Merson: 'He can put a ball on someone's head from 50 yards.'

MODEL Jodie Kidd: 'Even if he retired tomorrow, he's a legend.'

GARY Lineker: 'I think you can already say he's one of our best-ever players.'

MICHAEL Owen: 'I don't think there's many players work as hard as David when he hasn't got the ball.'

* * *

Incredible though it may seem, the man who has a winning combination of good looks, a beautiful and successful wife, more money than he knows what to do with and the respect and admiration of his country… is also a down-to-earth bloke who effortlessly charms anyone he meets with his easy-going, friendly nature. And if you think that's too good to be true, here are a few tales from ordinary people who have had the luck to meet this extraordinary individual:

DAVID once left his wallet on the roof of his Mercedes after filling up with petrol and signing autographs and then forgot all about it and drove off. It contained credit cards, £520, and most precious of all, photographs of Victoria and Brooklyn. But the cashiers at the Trowell motorway services on the M1 near Nottingham spotted what had happened. Tammy Booth and Emma Murfin were watching in horror as the car swept away with the wallet still on the roof. Straight away, Tammy set off in pursuit – she walked down a slip road and soon found the wallet lying on the ground. The girls, who earn £4.51 an hour, handed the wallet in to the police. They were delighted to get a call a couple of days later from David Beckham to say thanks. 'I was gobsmacked when he came on the phone,' says Tammy. 'He said he didn't think he would get it back and I told him I would have done the same for anyone. It was just part of my job. Afterwards I just screamed at my boyfriend, "David Beckham has just rung me!" It's not every day you get a famous footballer ringing your home.' David made sure the girls got thank-you presents and ticket to a Manchester United game.

'CAN I PLAY A ROUND in flip-flops?'
That request – which came from none
other that David Beckham – startled the
young female assistant in the professional's
shop at an exclusive golf club near
Nottingham.

'I just couldn't believe what I was seeing,'
17-year-old Karen Clifford recalls, 'so I
wasn't really listening to what he was saying.
I was so astonished to see David Beckham
standing only a few feet away that I had to
pinch myself to make sure I was not
dreaming. He looked absolutely drop dead
gorgeous, much nicer than he seems on
television. I was just thinking My mum is
not going to believe this when he asked
again if he could go out on the course and
play in flip-flops. I didn't know what to say.
He was just standing there on his own in a
track suit and I looked down and saw that
on his feet he really was wearing flip-flops,
just an old pair, the sort you might wear on
the beach on your holidays. For me he
could play a round in whatever he liked, but
some of our members are very pernickety
about rules and regulations and I know they
wouldn't bend them, even for the captain of
the England football team.

'I think he could see I was a bit
embarrassed and tongue-tied, because he
smiled and said, "I hope it's not a problem."
I was flustered and I blurted out that I didn't

mind but that some members might object and also I tried to say that parts of the course are very hilly and uneven and he might slip. I must have sounded like a complete twerp, but he just smiled again and said, "It's OK, can I have some golf shoes then." He spoke so softly that the whole thing seemed unreal but I found myself selling a pair of golf shoes worth £125 to David Beckham. He got them and then hired some clubs and just as he was leaving he asked if we had any balls. We had quite a large stock and I pointed to them. He said, "Can I take them all please?" There were hundreds of balls in the shop and he took the lot. I've no idea why he wanted so many and I was too shy to ask. He smiled and paid and went out. I was left standing there with my jaw on the floor.

'I expected to see a camera crew come in and show me up for being a mug with a lookalike, but nothing happened. He was the real thing and he was a really nice bloke. I have never been interested in football before, but I have seen every game he has been in on television since.' (In fact, David says he gets more nervous playing golf than he does playing football in front of 65,000 people: 'I would rather run out naked at Old Trafford than stand up in front of four people playing golf.')

'IT WAS 2.30 am and my car broke down on the M6 north of Stoke,' recalls motorist Steve Davey. 'There was a horrible grinding noise and all the power just sort of drained away. I managed to coast onto the hard shoulder and got out into a pig of a rainy night and opened the bonnet. I'm not sure why, because I know nothing about cars – and this wasn't even my car. It was my boss's nearly new Mercedes and I was due to be at his place just off the M25 at 6 am. He had flown down from Manchester the previous day and I was catching him up to take him into work next day. I'd only had the job a couple of weeks after being out of work for ages, so I was desperate to make a big impression.

'There wasn't much traffic,' Steve continues, 'and I hadn't got a mobile so I was just setting off to walk to the next motorway phone when a sports car pulled up next to me. The window opened and a baseball cap leaned towards me and this guy said, "Have you got a problem, mate?" I said, "Yes, it just went dead", and I tried to look as helpless as possible. "Hop in," he said. "I'll call someone out." I stepped down into this flash car and I suddenly realised that this was a Ferrari and this was David Beckham driving it. I was so stunned, I blurted out "Bloody hell, you're D–" and he stopped me with a smile and said, "Don't start all that." Then he talked into the phone giving directions to where we were.

'I just started to thank him for stopping and he said, "That's fine, mate. Us night owls have got to stick together." And I sat there in the front of this fabulous car, with the England football captain, thinking, My mates are not going to believe this. I asked him where he was going at this time and he said, "Just driving. It unwinds me. I get the sounds turned up and just drive." A breakdown truck appeared behind us and two mechanics got out. They got my car going in about three minutes flat and then got back into their truck and drove on up the motorway.

'I turned to David Beckham open-mouthed and he just said, "Have this one on me." He smiled, got back into his car and drove off. I was left standing on the hard shoulder just gobsmacked. And I realised I hadn't even got his autograph. It seemed rude to ask when he clearly just wanted to be an ordinary guy. I got back in the car and drove back down to London and my boss was none the wiser about who had got his car fixed in the middle of the night. I am an Aston Villa fan, but from that night I will always have a soft spot for Man Utd, or whatever team David Beckham plays for. He's a gent.'

David admits to being far more nervous about playing golf in public than playing football – whether he's allowed to wear flip-flops or not!

'DAVID Beckham will always be my son Daniel's soccer idol,' says model Donna Giblin, 'and I was a heroine in Daniel's eyes the day I got David's autograph for him. Daniel and I were in the restaurant at the Marriott Worsley Park Hotel and Country Club, Worsley, Manchester, when I got up to get something from my car. As I walked back into the restaurant, I was followed in by David Beckham and the rest of the England team, who had been training for the game against Greece. Daniel couldn't believe it. I didn't know the team were there, but it looked as though I'd gone out to my car and then brought the entire England squad back in with me. The funny thing was that both Daniel and I were wearing Brooklyn sweaters – with the name Brooklyn on the front. It was too good an opportunity to miss and so I went up and politely asked David for his autograph, explaining that it really was sheer coincidence that we were wearing Brooklyn sweaters, that we hadn't put them on just for his benefit! He laughed then kindly signed his autograph. He was very happy to oblige.

'Oddly enough, that wasn't the first time I'd met him,' Donna reveals. 'That happened a few years earlier when I was doing some promotion work for Manchester United at Old Trafford. I was dressed in the Man U kit, throwing footballs into the crowd. In those days, Beckham was the baby of the squad and he was very friendly and charming. It was nice to find that, having gone on to such big fame and the captaincy of England, he was still friendly and equally charming.'

So there you have it. The man who has everything is also a genuinely nice guy. Critics take note.

CHAPTER 7

DID YOU HEAR THE ONE ABOUT DAVID BECKHAM...?

WITH ALL the pressures that go with being David Beckham, it must help that the man himself has a great sense of humour. He is a huge fan of David Jason and *Only Fools and Horses* and when he has been unable to get to sleep at nights, he has been known to stay up watching videos of Del Boy and the Peckham posse. And he enjoys a good laugh even when it is directed at him, so long as the jokes are funny. He loved laughing along with Victoria when they were subjected to merciless mickey-taking in his famous interview with Ali G. But he was very nervous before the recording. They knew that many celebrities have turned down the chance to confront the fast-talking, foul-mouthed comic, but this was for charity, for Red Nose Day on the BBC. Ali G had said he would do a special interview show for the night, but only if the BBC lined up either the Beckhams or the Clintons. David and Victoria are always keen to raise as much money as possible for charity and they duly agreed to the daunting appearance. The couple have had so much teasing from all directions since they sprang to prominence that they thought at least it would show that they didn't take themselves too seriously. They bravely faced up to a hilarious encounter with Ali G with all the gags very much at their expense. It was very crude and very funny, although some of David and Victoria's comical retorts were edited out of the final version.

David also enjoys the humour of multi-talented comedian Harry Enfield and particularly of impressionist Alistair McGowan. They've had many laughs at McGowan's sketch in which he plays David to Ronnie Ancona's Victoria. Both are sitting at their thrones for dinner. 'David' says to 'Victoria', 'Why are these peas still in the pod?' And 'Victoria' replies, 'They're mange tout, Dave.'

Many people might be surprised to discover that David Beckham loves David Beckham jokes. He often tells them himself. Here's a selection of his own favourites:

How do you change
David Beckham's mind?
Blow in his ear.

Why does Becks go out
when the lightning starts?
He thinks someone's
taking his picture.

How do you make
David Beckham laugh
on a Thursday?
Tell him a joke on Monday.

Why does David Beckham
stare at the orange juice
at breakfast?
Because it says
'Concentrate'.

What is the difference
between David Beckham
and an Airfix model?
One's a glueless kit…

David Beckham went to New York and was amazed at how big everything was. Checking into a hotel he asked where the loo was but took a wrong turning and walked straight into the swimming pool. As staff rushed in to help, David yelled:
'For God's sake don't flush it!'

What do you do if
David Beckham throws
a pin at you?
Run like mad, he's got a
grenade in his mouth.

What is the difference between David Beckham and a supermarket trolley? A supermarket trolley has a mind of its own.

David and Victoria are sitting watching the nine o'clock news when they see the main story is about a man threatening to hurl himself off Waterloo Bridge into the River Thames below. The man seems to be agonising over whether or not to jump as the police try to talk him down. David and Victoria are gripped and start arguing about whether he will jump or not. Victoria turns to David and says: 'David, I bet you £5,000 that he jumps.' David replies: '£5,000? Done. I bet that he doesn't.' They shake hands on the bet and watch with fascination as the man leaps from the bridge and down into the water. David takes out his wallet and hands a triumphant Victoria £5,000. But she refuses the money. Victoria says: 'I can't take your money, David. I was cheating. The truth is, I saw the six o'clock news so I knew he was going to jump.' 'No babe,' says David. 'That money is yours, fair and square. I was cheating just as much as you were. I was watching the six o'clock news too. I saw him jump, but I just didn't think he would do it again...'

Posh and David are riding home from Heathrow in a taxi after a trip. 'Where have you been?' asks the cheery cabbie. 'New York,' says David. 'We saw a show and did some shopping.' 'Did you have any nice meals,' asks the cabbie. 'Yes, one really great one,' says David.

'What was the name of the restaurant?' asks the cabbie. 'I don't know. I can't remember. Name some big railway stations in London,' says David. The cabbie starts: 'Waterloo, Paddington, Victoria...' 'That's it!' yells David. 'Victoria, what's the name of that restaurant we went to?'

David Beckham is so dim that he takes a ruler to bed to see how long he sleeps.

David Beckham thought Eartha Kitt was a set of garden tools.

David Beckham missed the number 44 bus, so he took the number 22 twice.

Gary Neville asks David
if he has ever seen Evita.
David says: 'I'm not sure.
Who does he play for?'

David Beckham is over the moon. He yells to Victoria: 'Three weeks and five days! Three weeks and five days!' Victoria asks him why he is so happy. He says: 'I've done this jigsaw in three weeks and five days!' 'Is that good?' asks Victoria. 'It's fantastic,' says David. 'It says three to five years on the box.'

The Manchester United players are all together after training when Ryan Giggs says to Alex Ferguson: 'Boss. There's a problem. I'm not playing on Saturday unless I get a cortisone injection.' David Beckham jumps to his feet and says: 'Hey listen here. If he's having a new car, so am I.'

David Beckham, Paul Scholes and Roy Keane are trapped on the second storey of a burning building. They rush onto the balcony and see firemen down below holding a blanket for them. 'Jump, jump,' they shout to Keane. He leaps off the balcony and at the last minute the firemen whip away the blanket and Keane smashes into the pavement as the firemen fall about laughing.

Then it is Scholes' turn. He hesitates but the firemen encourage him it will be all right and hold the blanket up again. Scholes jumps and the firemen do it again. They whip away the blanket and roar with laughter as Scholes goes splat onto the concrete. The firemen hold up the blanket to Beckham, who has watched all this in horror as flames lick at his heels. The firemen encourage Beckham to jump, but he says: 'I'm not jumping down there. If I do you'll whip away the blanket.' 'No, we won't,' say the firemen. 'I don't trust you,' says Beckham. 'Really, we won't do it to you,' say the firemen. David says: 'All right. But I don't trust you. I will jump into the blanket on one condition. You put that blanket down and step 10 yards away from it and put your hands behind your backs.'

David Beckham had a terrifying experience when he went riding the other day. He started off comfortably enough, but then the horse started bucking and rearing and lurching right out of control. David struggled to hang on, but it was no good. He was thrown off and crashed to the ground with one foot still stuck in the stirrups. David yelled anxiously for help but he was badly hurt and fading fast. There was a happy ending, though: the Woolworths manager came out at just the right time and switched the ride off.

Victoria went to the garage to get a dent on her car repaired and the mechanic decided to play a joke on her. He said: 'Oh no, madam, you don't need to worry about this dent. This car has been fitted with special self-repair body panels. If you blow hard up the exhaust pipe and the metal with the dent in will pop back into shape.' Victoria was delighted. She drove home and tried it. But the dent remained unmoved. David saw what she was doing from the house and yelled: 'You idiot, Victoria. You have to wind the windows up first.'

When David Beckham went shopping he spotted something he had never seen before. He asked the assistant in the kitchen department what it was and he replied: 'It's a Thermos flask, Mr Beckham.' 'What does it do?' asked David. The assistant explained: 'It keeps hot things hot and cold things cold.' David liked the sound of that, so he bought one. He took it with him to the next training session and proudly showed it to his team-mates. 'Here lads, look at this,' said Beckham, proudly holding up his new Thermos flask.' The lads are impressed, but they ask: 'What does it do, David?' 'It keeps hot things hot and cold things cold,' says David. 'And what have you got in it?' asks skipper Roy Keane. David Beckham replies enthusiastically: 'Two cups of coffee and a choc ice.'

David Beckham is going on a shopping trip to Paris. He gets on the plane and walks straight through the curtains and sits down in first class. He puts his hand luggage into the overhead compartment and sits down. The stewardess approaches him nervously and points out that he has only got an economy ticket yet he is sitting in first class. David stands up and snorts indignantly: 'Don't you know who I am?' and is clearly unwilling to move. The stewardess looks anxiously around and another passenger quietly approaches her with the words, 'Perhaps I can help. I am a psychiatrist.' 'Oh thank you, sir,' says the stewardess. The psychiatrist leans over and whispers something in David's ear. David instantly leaps up, grabs his hand luggage and walks back towards economy class. The stewardess watches in rapt admiration. 'That was fantastic,' she exclaims, 'you must be a brilliant psychiatrist.' 'Not really,' says the man. 'I just told him that first class wasn't going to Paris.'

In his after-the-match interview, David Beckham was explaining how he was trying to control his temper on the pitch. 'It was the boss's idea,' says David. 'He told me to count to ten every time I start feeling angry, but the technique is not perfect.' 'Doesn't it calm you down,' asked the interviewer. 'It's not that,' replies David. 'It's just that sometimes the match is over by the time I've finished.'

But to David Beckham's credit, he is more than able to tell jokes against himself. On a TV documentary he came out with a few of his own. David Beckham walks up to a Coke machine in a casino, puts some coins in and out pops a can of Coke. He puts some more coins into the machine and out pops a Lilt. He puts more coins in and out pops an Iced Tea. Then a man walks up behind him and says: 'Can I use the machine, please?' David replies: 'Go away. Can't you see I'm winning every time.' David's other favourite: David Beckham goes to the hairdresser wearing earphones and carrying his own personal CD. 'I'm sorry, sir,' says the hairdresser. 'But you will have to take those headphones off for me to cut your hair?' 'No, no you can't,' says David. 'It's a matter of life or death.' So the hairdresser is forced to cut round the headphones until curiosity gets the better of her and she gently lifts one earpiece so she can hear what David is listening to. 'She hears a voice repeating over and over again: 'Breathe in, breathe out.'

CHAPTER 8

TEN GREAT GOALS

An unforgettable 55-yard shot from inside his own half for Manchester United against Wimbledon at Selhurst Park in 1996. It was a remarkable goal in every way: it was a strike of incredible precision executed with extraordinary audacity. Very few players would have had either the vision or the confidence in their own ability even to try and score from that distance. Beckham's long-range goal has been shown over and over again on TV all over the world and is acknowledged as one of soccer's most memorable moments. It eclipses legendary Brazilian Pele's frequently shown effort from the halfway line in the 1970 World Cup, which just missed, and former Tottenham star Nayim's 40-yard lob that sank Arsenal in the European Cup Winners Cup Final in Paris in 1994. (In the Channel 4 programme *The Hundred Greatest Sporting Moments*, David's famous goal came 18th.)

JOHNNY WILKINSON: England's record-breaking Rugby Union fly half: 'When I saw that goal from the halfway line, I knew just how much practice he had put in to get it right. I thought to myself, *Just how many balls did he have to hit in practice to get it right on the day?* Hundreds and hundreds. He'd have to be getting every one in, every time, on the practice field to be able to strike it like that in a match situation and score. Brilliant.'

ANGUS DEAYTON: 'People don't really do that outside of comic books.'

JAMES NESBITT star of *Cold Feet* : 'It was one of those things that sent a call round the land and the world that some boy had arrived.'

JOHN MOTSON: BBC commentator: 'That may go down as one of the great goals of our time.'

The 93rd minute last-gasp free-kick for England against Greece which curled into the top right corner of the net in 2001. Not only was it a brilliant free-kick, it was a goal scored under the most intense pressure. The final whistle was just seconds away, England's hopes of automatic qualification for the World Cup rested on Beckham's kick going in to ensure a 2-2 draw, and the England skipper had already failed with several free-kick attempts on goal earlier in the game.

A powerful snap shot from outside the penalty area to open the scoring against Arsenal at Villa Park in the 1999 FA Cup quarter-final. David swivelled and struck a right foot shot that curled away from David Seaman's despairing right hand. It was a magnificent goal in a thrilling cup tie that put Manchester United on the way to a 2-1 win, on the way to Wembley, and eventually to the second part of the Treble.

A surging run at pace and a searing shot from outside the penalty area, cutting his foot across the ball, to send it swerving high into the net against Tottenham Hotspur in 1996. It was an outstanding goal in its own right, but all the more memorable for Beckham in that it was against Spurs and came just a week after his brilliant free-kick against them had knocked the London club out of the 5th round of the FA Cup.

A vital equaliser against Tottenham Hotspur at Old Trafford on May 16, 1999, which helped Manchester United to an eventual 2-1 win that clinched the Premiership title, the first trophy in their incredible Treble of that year. It was a desperately needed goal just before half-time, after Les Ferdinand had given Spurs the lead with a freakish looping goal. Beckham received the ball out to the right side of the penalty area and unleashed a powerful shot across Ian Walker's goal into the top corner.

Beckham's first goal for England, an arcing free-kick into the top corner against Colombia in the World Cup France '98. Another perfectly executed free-kick, and the perfect answer to England manager Glenn Hoddle who had excluded Beckham from the England team at the start of the tournament.

The winner against Chelsea in an FA Cup semi-final 2-1 victory at Villa Park in 1996. It was the goal that took Manchester United to Wembley. A mistake by Burley left Beckham clean through the Chelsea defence and he calmly advanced on goal and stroked the ball home.

An impudent lob against Newcastle at Wembley in the Charity Shield match in 1996. Beckham darted forward behind the Newcastle defence and deftly lifted the ball over the goalkeeper.

The winning goal in a 1-0 defeat of Liverpool in 1996. Beckham seized on a loose ball and drove it fiercely past David James into the bottom left-hand corner.

A glorious trademark free-kick against Manchester City at Maine Road, the only goal of the game. The ball flew over City's wall of defenders and into goalkeeper Nicky Weaver's net at a fierce pace. Not only was it a fine goal, it was a goal of crucial importance – the winning goal in a derby game against deadly rivals Manchester City on City's own turf. United's home town rivals had just returned to the top flight for the first time after many years spent languishing outside the Premiership.

DAVID BECKHAM FACTFILE

Born: David Robert Joseph Beckham
Birthplace: Leytonstone, East London
Date of Birth: May 2, 1975
Height: 6ft 0in
Married: Spice Girl Victoria Adams, July 4, 1999
Son: Brooklyn, born March 1999

Manchester United

- Scouted by Manchester United while playing right wing for Waltham Forest Under-12s against Redbridge.

- Won Bobby Charlton TSB Soccer Skills Final held at Old Trafford, December 1986.

- Appeared as United mascot at Upton Park for the 1987 game West Ham v Manchester United.

- Signed as Manchester United trainee: July 8, 1991.

- Senior Manchester United debut: at age 17, came on as a sub replacing Andrei Kanchelskis v Brighton in Rumbelows League Cup tie v Brighton and Hove Albion: September 23, 1992.

- Signed as Manchester United professional: January 23, 1993.

- Champions' League debut: Scored on debut v Turkish club Galatasaray: December 7, 1994.

- Loaned out to Preston North End for five matches and scored on debut, directly from a corner kick, for Preston v Doncaster.

- Manchester United League debut v Leeds United: April 2, 1995.

- First Premiership goal for Manchester United v Aston Villa, 1995.

Honours With Manchester United

1992 FA Youth Cup – winner

1993 FA Youth Cup – runner-up

1994 Reserve Team Championship

1996 FA Premier League – Championship

1996 FA Cup – winner

1996 FA Charity Shield – winner

1997 FA Premier League – Championship

1997 FA Charity Shield – winner

1999 FA Premier League – Championship

1999 FA Cup – winner

1999 UEFA European Champions Cup – winner

2000 FA Premier League – Championship

2001 FA Premier League – Championship

England International Honours

Youth international.

Under-21 international: 1994/96.

Full England international – First cap England v Moldova: September 1, 1996.

First England goal v Colombia in World Cup: June 26, 1998.

Appointed by England coach Kevin Keegan as vice-captain of England for the World Cup qualifying game against Germany: October 7, 2000.

Appointed captain of England v Italy, by caretaker England coach Peter Taylor: November 15, 2000.

Appointed captain of England by new national coach Sven-Goran Eriksson for England v Spain: February 28, 2001.

First goal as England captain in 2-1 win over Finland in World Cup qualifier: March 24, 2001.

Individual Honours

1997 Professional Footballers Association Young Player Of The Year.

1997 Professional Footballers Association Player Of The Year runner-up.

1999 UEFA Best Midfielder.

2000 FIFA World Footballer Of The Year runner-up.

2000 European Footballer Of The Year runner-up.

2000 BBC Sports Personality Of The Year runner-up.

2001 BBC TV Sports Personality Of The Year.

2001 World Footballer Of The Year runner-up.

2001 Voted ManUtd.com's Player of the Year for the season 2000/01, receiving more than a quarter of the votes. (More than 94,000 fans all over the world voted in the poll on the official website.)

League Record

Season	Games	Goals
1994/95	2	0
1995/96	33	7
1996/97	36	8
1997/98	37	9
1998/99	34	6
1999/2000	31	9

The authors gratefully acknowledge the
following people and sources who helped
in the preparation of this tribute. We have
attempted to be as inclusive as possible,
but if we have inadvertently left anybody
out, then we apologise:

John and Tyna Airey, Neil Ashwood,
BBC Manchester, BBC TV, Blakeway
Productions, Cindy Blanchflower, Rob and
Les Braithwaite, John and Pippa Burmester,
Eric Butler, Carlton TV, Ellis Cashmore,
Channel 4, Channel 5, the Daily Express, the
Daily Mail, the Daily Telegraph, Kenny Davey,
Roger Davis, John 'Five-goals' Dickinson,
Pat Foley, FHM, Donna and Dan Giblin,
Rod and Joy Gilchrist, Granada TV,
Dr Mark Giffiths, Richard Hall,
Chris Haynes, Kay Hurley, Tony Hyde,
Clive Jackson, Jerry Johns, John Killeen,
Alan Kingston, David Knight, Frank and
Hazel Langan, David Lingard,
Richard Littlejohn, London Weekend
Television, John Lowe, Match Of The Day,
Charles McCutcheon, Steve Mikkelson,
the Mirror, the News Of The World,
Now magazine, Michael Parkinson, the
People, Jim Randall, Rich and Famous,
Graham Riggall, Steve Savage, John Scott,
Sky Sports, Shoot magazine, the Sun, the
Sunday Mirror, Richard Turner, the Times,
Gordon Webb, Chris White, Dave White

Special thanks to Oliver Ewbank for his
statistical research.

The publishers are grateful to the following for permission to print the pictures contained in this book

ALPHA
Pages 20, 50, 57, 90, 100, 103, 146, 172/173; Colour section pages 1, 4, 5, 6

CAMERA PRESS
Pages 29, 34/5, 38, 44/45, 64, 111, 128, 131, 134, 142, 152, 154, 155; Colour section page 7

EXPRESS NEWSPAPERS
Pages 54, 70/71, 82/83, 84, 85, 88/9, 167

MATRIX
Page 73

MIRROR SYNDICATION
Page 86

NEWS INTERNATIONAL
Pages 62, 138

PA PHOTOS
Pages 76/7, 171

POPPERFOTO
Pages 114/115, 116/117

REX FEATURES
Pages 10, 13, 24, 41, 58, 98, 102, 106, 122, 150, 162, 163, 189, 197, 205, 236, 239, 243, 248; Colour section pages 2, 3, 8

SIMON MURPHY
Page 80